The Wall. Figures. Facts

Alexandra Hildebrandt

D1666020

The Wall.
Figures. Facts

Alexandra Hildebrandt

This book is an attempt to compile the facts and figures about the wall. The reappraisal of the GDR-past, however, is not finished by any means. Therefore we ask you to excuse any possible incompleteness in this edition.

Die Deutsche Bibliothek – CIP-Einheitsaufnahme

Hildebrandt Alexandra:
The Wall. Figures. Facts / Alexandra Hildebrandt
Berlin : Verl. Haus am Checkpoint Charlie, 2nd ed. 2005
ISBN 3-922484-53-0

© Verlag Haus am Checkpoint Charlie, Berlin
Friedrichstr. 43–45, 10969 Berlin, phone: +49 (0) 30-253725-0
Editorial office: Mauermuseum - Museum Haus am Checkpoint Charlie
Graphic design: Mauermuseum - Museum Haus am Checkpoint Charlie
Print, scans, lithographies: DMP Digital- & Offsetdruck GmbH, Berlin
Printed in Germany

ISBN 3-922484-53-0

TABLE OF CONTENTS

FOREWORD

By Rainer Hildebrandt
14.12.1914 - 09.01.2004

Will the Berlin Wall ever reach symbol status like the Wall of Troy, like the Wailing Wall or the Chinese Wall?

Under the impression of the German-German embraces and the tears about this sudden stroke of luck on November 9, 1989, many realised for the first time ever just how much the wall had separated us. A political construction that divided a country and a city became a challenge for artists and the activists of the first hour as well as for escape aids who faced the risk of many years of imprisonment if their plan failed.

Keith Haring painted about 100 meters of the wall with its yellowish prime with black and red matchstick men. The press reported "Opposition against the separation. Graffiti-artist painted Berlin Wall." One year before that Richard Hambleton created his "Colour Symphony", which he titled "Who's afraid of black-red-yellow?"

"Even the Vopos laughed", titled the West German press when Peter Lenk installed his "Mauer-Kieker" (wall watchers) on the Kennedy-podium. The two Frenchmen Thierry Noir and Christophe Bouchet, both residing in Berlin, painted several kilometres of the wall. It was not specific images but the richness of colour of the seamless "largest concrete canvas of the world" that made the wall famous, from Wim Wender's film "Der Himmel über Berlin" (The Sky over Berlin) up to the one hundred metre frieze by Keith Haring.

THE WALL will one day be written with capital letters. It consisted of the back wall, an electric contact fence, observation towers, bunkers, expanded metal fences, tank barriers, dog installations, metal tip mats, "wall towards the enemy". These were the elements, manufactured with German thoroughness, of the "best border safeguarding system in the world" (said the GDR army general Hoffmann).
Since 1971, the inner-German border was further perfected with automatic firing devices. These had a "dum-dum character". The square-cut steel cubes, 100 of which were contained in each firing funnel, caused "unnecessary suffering and irreparable damages". Several people who survived the injuries caused by these automatic firing devices have the sharp-edged and pointy steel splinters in their bodies for life, because a surgical removal would be too risky.

"Border violators are to be detected, arrested or destroyed", were the words of the instruction text for the daily border deployment. But the yearning for freedom was more intense than the fear. Over 400,000 people escaped across the wall and the inner-German border at the risk of death.
The border regime of the GDR claimed no less than 1,067 lives until 1989.

During a gathering of survivors of the resistance against Hitler, the former Senator of the Interior, Heinrich Albertz, said in 1962: "Since August 13, things have happened in the city about which we will not be able to speak openly for many years to come. Young people, whose names I am not allowed to mention, but which should one day be placed on a commemorative plaque, gave their lives for others without any order, fame or reward: in the sewers of this city, in tunnels dug with eternal effort, before the barbed wire of the dreadful tyranny, often with their bare hands opposite the machine guns of a criminal system. The history of German resistance will be continued in a new form."

The top athlete Harry Seidel channelled GDR-citizens. He approached people crying at the border fence, had them give him an address and brought the missing persons through the barbed wire at night at a place he had spied out. The platoon sergeant of the GDR-army, Rudi Thurow, saw himself forced to fire in the direction of his own people in order to save escapees from being fired at and in order to join them. (A few days later he went back to the same spot in order to call over to his soldiers that he did not aim directly at them. The point was to force them to take cover in order to save the lives of these escapees). It was the Berlin physics student Reinhard Furrer who organised the arrival and the protection of people willing to escape with imperious constructiveness and took over the most dangerous task – receiving the people willing to escape – himself. "You can only be helped if you become an astronaut", said a friend. He did.

"Scarlet Pimpernel" was the undercover name of another escape agent in commemoration of the French revolution, which freed many. Hasso Herschel has meanwhile become world famous. He did not stop until he had channelled the thousandth person.

Numerous of the activists that engaged themselves against the wall and the German division came to the anniversary of the construction of the wall or that of the day when Peter Fechter died. He wanted to escape and was already on top of the wall when he was shot at and deadly wounded. Most of the time the demonstrators used the border crossing point for foreigners, Checkpoint Charlie, as the place of their protests. Here, where diplomats moved between West and East Berlin, was the most likely spot to ensure that their campaigns raised public awareness while they were protected at the same time, but also because of the fact that the political pressure on the GDR was most effective here.

The Italian Gino Ragno came every year on the anniversary of the construction of the wall with a group of the Society for Italian-German Friendship, whose president he was. With the sign "There is no Unity in Europe without freedom for Berlin", the group dared to cross the border in order to affix the sign. This was met with a lot of applause from West Berlin.

After 15 minutes, an alarm commando came and removed the sign while the West Berliners were booing (August 13, 1964).

In December of 1965, Ragno together with other Italians placed a candle at the nearby Peter-Fechter-Memorial that the Roman bishop Bucco had blessed: "This candle shall be the symbol of peace that will prosper where the forces of unification are stronger than those of separation." Prior to that Ragno was granted an audience with Pope Paul VI. During this audience the Pope prayed for a "united, free and Christian Germany".

On August 7, 1986, the American citizen John Runnings (68) walked almost 500 m on top of THE WALL. During the 70 minutes, he also knocked out a piece of THE WALL. Visitors brought it to a museum. Runnings: "I am a carpenter and have fed my family with this work, but I am also a philosopher. I will show you Berliners how to influence THE WALL politically. As long as military threats are only answered with military responses, this does not change a thing." The public reacted very controversial. When John Runnings finally used a ladder of the GDR border troops to climb down to them, he was arrested and interrogated but released after 20 hours. In 1989, John Running built a battering ram, however, the West Berlin police confiscated this before he could use it at the wall. Runnings was arrested by GDR guards several times, but always expelled again pretty quickly. The GDR shied away from international conflict.

Since 1981, the philosopher Joseph Werner had conducted a vigil every year on each August 13th. He handed little black flags to visitors as a symbol of mourning for the Germans on the other side of the wall.

The Ghandi-follower Carl-Wolfgang Holzapfel demonstrated against THE WALL and the barbed wire already during the first weeks of the construction of THE WALL. In freezing temperatures he conducted hunger strikes and cautioned the people travelling to the Leipzig trade fair not to forget the people that were shot to death during escape attempts. In 1964, he tried to enter East Berlin with a banner that read "Freedom for Political Prisoners!" On his first two attempts he was turned back at the border crossing point Heinrich-Heine-Straße. Upon his third attempt at Checkpoint Charlie, he was arrested and sentenced to eight years in jail, but was ransomed by the Federal Republic of Germany after 13 months.

On August 13, 1989, Holzapfel lay – wrapped in a West German flag – for three hours on the white border line before he was taken away by West German policemen after these had been debating a long time with the East German border guards. He said he wanted to demonstrate that Berlin, that Germany remained a whole.

Still on January 19, 1989, head of state and party Erich Honekker declared: "The wall…will still be here in 50 and even in 100 years if the causes for it have not been abolished."

But its end was near without anyone realising just how near. The resistance against the injustice in the GDR and THE WALL saw its peak in the Leipzig "Monday Demonstrations" that started at the end of September 1989 with 8,000 demonstrators. One month later, the number had grown to 300,000 people who demonstrated for freedom and democratic rights and faced thousands of "security" and police forces.

The "Monday Demonstrations" kicked off an avalanche of liberation and even the Soviet Union, built upon millions of murdered people, came to an end without any bloody escalations. From victory to victory the non-violent struggles for freedom intensified in Eastern Europe with the end of the Berlin WALL thanks to non-violent solidarity.

People who were living in imprisonment made the experience that their desires come true in the most beautiful dreams. Sometimes these dreams are similar to each other: being united with the loved one, everything that used to separate has gone by, happiness in a colourful, warming brightness. In the few hours of one single night, the night of November 9th, 1989, a dream and at the same time a political utopia became reality. Never before did so many people say: "…but this is insane!" Here and there strangers hugging each other in the turmoil. Happiness had reached the absolute limit. Others cried because they thought of dear ones who could no longer experience this. Too many had to die in the trenches so that others could later march on victoriously. They have co-written the history of THE WALL and the separation of Germany. Through them THE WALL with all its horrible consequences and its non-violent overcoming has become a phenomenon.

Berlin, 2001

FIGURES

Berlin-Tiergarten,
ruin of the Reichstag, 1946

The Victims of the Second World War

The Victims of the Second World War[1]

Country	Lives lost
Soviet Union:	20.6 millions, of those 7 million civilians (official statement of the Soviet Union)
Germany:	5.25 millions, of those 500 000 civilians
Poland:	4.52 millions, of those 4.2 million civilians; additionally 1.5 million in the Polish eastern territories annexed by the Soviet Union in 1939
Japan:	1.8 million, of those 600 000 civilians
Yugoslavia:	1.69 million, of those 1,28 million civilians
France:	810 000, of those 470 000 civilians
Hungary:	420 000, of those 280 000 civilians
Great Britain:	386 000, of those 62 000 civilians
Rumania:	378 000
Italy:	330 000
USA:	259 000
The Netherlands:	210 000, of those 198 000 civilians
Greece:	160 000, of those 140 000 civilians
Belgium:	88 000, of those 76 000 civilians
Finland:	84 000
Bulgaria:	20 000
Norway:	10 000
Denmark:	1 400
China:	Unknown
Total losses:	Around 55 million dead

[1] See „Der Große Ploetz. Die Daten-Enzyklopädie der Weltgeschichte, 32., revised edition, Freiburg im Breisgau 2000, p. 802; contained therein is the estimated number of 4.2–5.7 million mainly non-German murdered Jews, see there, p. 900.

Soviet monument in Berlin-Treptow

British military cemetery at Heerstraße in Berlin-Charlottenburg

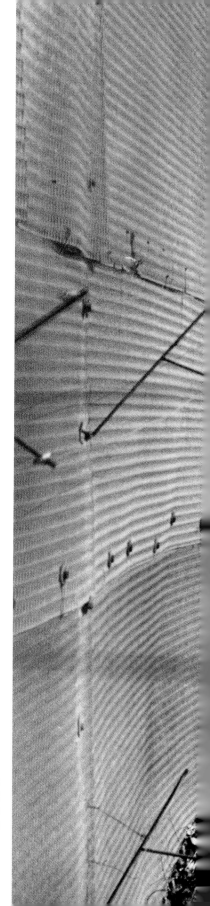

Metal lattice fence with
automatic firing devices
at the inner-German
border, around 1980

The Division
of Germany

Border crossing point Herrenburg near Lübeck, May 1952

Inner-German border between Bavaria and Thuringia near Heinersdorf, 1959

Construction of a new wall in the Thuringian-Bavarian town of Mödlareuth, separated by the border, April 1966

View over the newly erected concrete wall in Blankenstein, September 1972

The Western Occupied Zones 1945–1949[1]

Occupied Zone	Inhabitants	Area in km²	States
American	16.7 million	116 670	Bavaria
			Bremen
			Hesse
			Wuerttemberg-Baden
British	22.7 million	97 300	Hamburg
			Lower Saxony
			North Rhine-Westphalia
			Schleswig-Holstein
French	5.8 million	39 000	Rhineland-Palatinate
			Saarland
			South Baden
			Wuerttemberg-Hohenzollern
Total	45.2 million	252 970	

[1] See H. Dollinger and Th. Vogelsang (publishers), „Deutschland unter den Besatzungsmächten 1945–1949", Munich 1967, p. 148.

The Soviet Occupied Zone 1945–1949[1]

Occupied zone	Inhabitants	Area in km²	States
Soviet	17.8 million	121 600	Brandenburg
			Mecklenburg-West Pomerania
			Saxony
			Saxony-Anhalt
			Thuringia

[1] See Dollinger, Vogelsang, "Deutschland," p. 148; not contained therein Berlin with 3.2 million inhabitants and an area size of 900 km².

The Course of the Border between the FRG and the GDR[1]

State	Border length in km	Border share in %
Schleswig-Holstein incl. 15 km of Baltic Sea border	151	10.9
Lower Saxony	550	39.5
Hesse	268	19.3
Bavaria	422	30.3
Total	1 391	100.0

[1] See B. Irmscher and D. Moldmann, „Am Deutsch-Deutschen Rand. Landschaft, Geschichte, Kultur, Wirtschaft entlang einer 1240 km Reiseroute am östlichen Rand der Bundesrepublik", Hamburg [1989], p. 21, 45, 114, 143.

The Inner-German Border Crossings[1]

Border crossing	Border town FRG	Zone boundary	Border town GDR	Admitted traffic
B 104	Lübeck-Schlutup	British/Soviet	Selmsdorf	Exchange and transit traffic of passengers and goods, not to and from Berlin (West)
B 5	Lauenburg	British/Soviet	Horst	Exchange and transit traffic of passengers and goods
Autobahn	Gudow	British/Soviet	Zarrentin	Exchange and transit traffic of passengers and goods
B 71	Bergen (Dumme)	British/Soviet	Salzwedel	Exchange traffic of passengers
Autobahn checkpoint Alpha	Helmstedt	British/Soviet	Marienborn	Exchange and transit traffic of passengers and goods
B 247	Duderstadt	British/Soviet	Worbis	Exchange traffic of passengers
Autobahn	Herleshausen	American/Soviet	Wartha	Exchange and transit traffic of passengers and goods
B 19	Eußenhausen	American/Soviet	Meiningen	Exchange traffic of passengers
B 4	Rottenbach	American/Soviet	Eisfeld	Exchange traffic of passengers
Autobahn	Rudolphstein	American/Soviet	Hirschberg	Exchange and transit traffic of passengers and goods
Railway	Lübeck	British/Soviet	Herrnburg	Exchange and transit traffic of passengers and goods, not to and from Berlin (West)
Railway	Büchen	British/Soviet	Schwanheide	Exchange and transit traffic of passengers and goods
Railway	Wolfsburg	British/Soviet	Oebisfelde	Exchange and transit passenger traffic, not to and from Berlin (West); exchange and transit traffic of goods
Railway	Helmstedt	British/Soviet	Marienborn	Exchange and transit traffic of passengers and goods
Railway	Walkenried	British/Soviet	Ellrich	Exchange and transit traffic of goods
Railway	Bebra	American/Soviet	Gerstungen	Exchange and transit traffic of passengers and goods
Railway	Ludwigsstadt	American/Soviet	Probstzella	Exchange and transit traffic of passengers and goods
Railway	Hof	American/Soviet	Gutenfürst	Exchange and transit traffic of passengers and goods
Elbe river	Schnackenburg	British/Soviet	Cumlosen	Exchange and transit traffic of goods
Mittellandkanal	Rühen	British/Soviet	Buchhorst	Exchange and transit traffic of goods

[1] Status: 1989; see P. J. Lapp, „Gefechtsdienst im Frieden. Das Grenzregime der DDR 1945-1990", Bonn 1999, p. 95 and „Frontdienst im Frieden. Die Grenztruppen der DDR. Entwicklung, Struktur, Aufgaben", Koblenz 1986 (= Bernard & Graefe current, vol. 45), p. 224 pp.

The Components of the Safeguarding System at the Inner-German Border[1]

Type of installation		Status at the end of the year					
		1963	1965	1967	1969	1971	1973
Double-row metal lattice fence (mines in the gap)	km			79	304	494	708
Single-row metal lattice fence with automatic firing devices	km					61	82
Double-row metal lattice fence (mines in the gap)	km	1 133	1 176	1 466	1 142	1 083	604
Old, simple barbed wire fence (mostly dilapidated)	km	512	344				
Mine field strip	km	778	722	778	846	798	710
Mines (app.)	no.			1,6 Mio.	1,8 Mio.	1,7 Mio.	1,6 Mio.
Car trenches (fortified with concrete slabs)	km			349	367	345	345
Car trenches (w/o concrete slabs)	km	658	439	137	162	208	376
Convoy paths (not concreted)	km			749	797	728	518
Convoy paths (concreted)	km			41	112	220	534
Observation towers (concrete)[2]	no.			k. A.	40	154	244
Observation towers (wood)	no.	448	473	1189	476	389	297
Observation platforms in trees	no.	80	112	133	138	129	125
Observation bunkers (concrete)	no.	531	516	665	687	701	712
Ground observation stands	no.	169	693	544	286	262	186
Dog installations	no.			259	354	346	457
Dogs	no.			343	467	480	676
Light barriers	km			82	143	164	157
Number of light barriers	km			68	94	111	111
Protection strip with electric and acoustic signal installations	km						416
Strip for collection of evidence	km			ca. 1 300	ca. 1 300	ca. 1 300	ca. 1 300
10 m control strip	km	1 179	690				

Type of installation		Status at the end of the year				
		1977	1980	1983	1986	1989[3]
Metal lattice fence	km	1 141	1 277,2	1 283,1	1 270,8	1 265,0
Double barbed wire fence	km	256	72,6	45,6	20,6	
Protective strip fence	km	880	1 111,6	1 160,4	1 207,2	1 189,9
Mine fields	km	433	232,1	154,4		
Border section with automatic firing devices	km	291	410,6	439[4]		
Concrete restraining wall/screens	km	14	25,6	29,7	30,2	29,0
Car trenches	km	771	832,0	837,7	837,7	822,2
Convoy/patrol paths	km	1 228	1 321,3	1 336,5	1 334,3	1 336,7
Light barriers	km	229	253,3	241,3	249,1	228,2
Ground bunkers (dugouts)	no.	991	835	786	663	394
Observation towers (concrete/brickwork)	no.	455	645	667	638	453
Observation towers (wood/steel)	no.	121	68	46	34	108
Dog installations	km	79	88,1	86,6	95,8	57,2
Dogs	no.	985	974	1 063	1 143	696

[1] See L. Dierske (reviser), „Die Geschichte des Bundesgrenzschutzes", vol. 2: from 1963 to 1973, Bonn [1975], p. 359 and activity report of the German Border Police (BGS) 1978-1989, published by the press department at the Ministry of the Interior, Bonn 1979-1990.
[2] As of 1966 erection of mushroom-shaped observation towers, as of 1975 erection of angular ones; see Lapp, "Gefechtsdienst im Frieden", l. c., p. 243 and J. Ritter and P. J. Lapp, "Die Grenze. Ein deutsches Bauwerk", Berlin 1997, p. 110.
[3] Status: 9.11.1989.
[4] Target date: 31.8.1983; afterwards dismantling of the automatic firing devices (SM-70).

Demarcation line with concrete watchtower near Zorge/Harz, July 1969

British sector,
Tauentzienstraße
with Gedächtnis-
kirche, early
summer of 1945

The Division of Berlin

Bernauer Straße at the corner of Schwedter Straße. Border patrols guard the sector boundary, August 13, 1961

Armed customs officers at the Brandenburg Gate, 1963

Achtung!
Sie verlassen nach 40m West-Berlin

East Berliners (in the background) waving to their relatives and friends in the west sector (foreground), garden colony Schönholz (Berlin-Pankow).

A look to the west through a window secured with barbed wire to avoid escape attempts.
Bernauer Straße, September 1961

The Western Sectors[1]

Sector	Area in km²	Districts
American	210.9	Kreuzberg Neukölln Schöneberg Steglitz Tempelhof Zehlendorf
British	169.3	Charlottenburg Spandau Tiergarten Wilmersdorf
French	104.9	Reinickendorf Wedding
Total	485.1	

[1] See „Berlin Handbuch. Das Lexikon der Bundeshauptstadt", Berlin 1992, p. 134, 1050.

The East Sector[1]

Sector	Area in km²	Districts
Soviet	403.4	Friedrichshain Hellersdorf (since 1986) Hohenschönhausen (since 1985) Köpenick Lichtenberg Marzahn (since 1979) Mitte Pankow Prenzlauer Berg Treptow Weißensee

[1] See Berlin Handbuch, Berlin, l. c., p. 134, 550, 566, 804, 1050.

The Population Development in Berlin[1]

Year	Berlin (West)	Berlin (East)
1945	1 733 605	1 073 799
1946	2 012 532	1 174 582
1950	2 146 952	1 189 074
1960	2 202 241	1 071 775
1970	2 122 346	1 086 374
1980	1 896 230	1 152 529
1989	2 134 051	1 279 212

[1] See C. Schwartau, „Berlin-Statistik", in: G. Langguth (publisher) „Berlin vom Brennpunkt der Teilung zur Brücke der Einheit", Cologne 1990, p. 479–493, here p. 480.

Border soldiers during the
assembly of the barbed wire fence
on top of the wall, Chausseestraße
(district of Mitte/Wedding),
September 1962

The Wall

In many places, the barbed wire fences were reinforced by a wall under close surveillance, August 1961

Conscripted "building soldiers" guarded by members of the People's Army, Checkpoint Charlie, December 1961

Water cannons
deployed
against western
photographers,
Brandenburg
Gate,
August 1961

American
solders and
GDR border
soldiers facing
each other at
the wall in
Kreuzberg/
Mitte,
December 1961

The Frontier Line in and around Berlin[1]

Area	Sector boundary in km	Border to the GDR in km	Total in km
Berlin (total)	45,9 (1989: 43,1)	232,0 (1989: 229,3)	277,9 (1989: 272,4)
Berlin (West)	45,9 (1989: 43,1)	114,6 (1989: 111,9)	160,5 (1989: 155,0)
Berlin (East)	45,9 (1989: 43,1)	117,4	163,3 (1989: 160,5)

District	Sector boundary in km	Border to the GDR in km	Total in km
Berlin (West)			
Kreuzberg	8.7		
Wedding	7.2		
Tiergarten	4.8		
Spandau		33.8	
Zehlendorf		26.3	
Tempelhof		12.2	
Steglitz		7.2	
Neukölln	15.6	9.1	24.7
Reinickendorf	9.6	26.0	35.6
Berlin (East)			
Treptow	17.1		
Mitte	13.6		
Pankow	10.9		
Prenzlauer Berg	2.3		
Friedrichshain	2.0		

District of exclaves belonging to Berlin (West)	Exclave	Border to the GDR in km
Zehlendorf	Wüste Mark	2.2
	Steinstücken	1.7
Spandau	Fichtewiesen	1.0
	Erlengrund	0.3
Total		5.2

Frontier line according to utilisation area	in km
On railroad embankments, through fields, swampy areas and similar	55.0
Mainly through residential areas	37.0
Through forest areas (app.)	30.0
Through watercourses, lakes and canals	24.0
Mainly through industrial areas	16.5
Total[2]	162.5

Type of restrictedly accessible or completely blocked roads, August 13, 1961	Number
Autobahn	1
Federal roads	6
Main roads	37
Country and side roads	149
Completely blocked roads in the sectors area	55
Completely blocked roads in the area along the East German border	129
Cut-up or blocked squares (Hindenburgplatz, Potsdamer Platz, Mariannenplatz, Lohmühlenplatz)	4

[1] Status 1962; see „Ulbrichts Mauer. Zahlen, Fakten, Daten", published by the Federal Ministry for All-German Questions, 3rd rev. and augm. ed., Bonn 1962, p. 4 pp. and p. 9; the figures for 1989 after different territory exchanges between Bln. (W) and Bln. (E) as well as the GDR; see "Die Mauer und ihr Fall", published by the Press and Information Office of the State of Bln., 5th, augm. ed., Berlin 1992, p. 20 and "Berlin Handbuch", Berlin, l. c., p. 435 pp.
[2] On 2 km border section through watercourses that were important industrial installations at the same time, therefore 2 km too much in total.

Frontier line between Berlin-Rudow and the district of Königs Wusterhausen, view towards Waltersdorfer Chaussee, June 1968

Frontier line along Bethaniendamm in Kreuzberg, Mach 1972

The Border Crossing Points in and around Berlin[1]

Street border crossings Berlin (West) — Berlin (East)[2]	Sector Crossing	Destination
Bornholmer Straße	French/ Soviet	Exchange traffic of GDR-citizens, residents of Berlin (West) and the FRG with and without car
Chausseestraße	French/ Soviet	Exchange traffic of GDR-citizens and residents of Berlin (West) with and without car
Invalidenstraße	British/ Soviet	Exchange traffic of GDR-citizens and residents of Berlin (West) with and without car
Friedrichstraße Checkpoint Charlie	American/ Soviet	Foreigners, allies and diplomatic personnel
Prinzenstraße/Heinrich-Heine-Straße	American/ Soviet	Exchange traffic of GDR-citizens and citizens of the FRG as well as diplomatic personnel
Oberbaumbrücke	American/ Soviet	Exchange traffic of GDR-citizens and residents of Berlin (West), pedestrians only
Sonnenallee	American/ Soviet	Exchange traffic of GDR-citizens and residents of Berlin (West) with and without car

[1] Status: 1989; see Lapp, „Gefechtsdienst im Frieden", l. c., p. 148 pp. and „Innerdeutsche Beziehungen. Die Entwicklung der Beziehungen zwischen der Bundesrepublik Deutschland und der Deutschen Demokratischen Republik 1980–1986". A documentation published by the Federal Ministry for Inner-German Relations, Bonn 1986, p. 110 pp. A survey of the type of limited accessible and completely blocked roads as of August 13, 1961; see "Ulbrichts Mauer", l.c., p. 9.

[2] See notice by the Ministry of the Interior of the GDR about the access to Berlin (East) of August 12, 1961, in: „Dokumente zur Deutschlandpolitik" IV/7 (1961), p. 8 pp. and the road crossing points Kopenhagener Straße, Wollankstraße, Bornholmer Straße, Brunnenstraße, Chausseestraße, Brandenburger Tor, Friedrichstraße, Heinrich-Heine-Straße, Oberbaumbrücke, Puschkin-Allee, Elsenstraße, Sonnenallee and Rudower Straße listed therein; see also notice by the Ministry of the Interior of the GDR about the access to Berlin (East) of August 22, 1961, in: V. Koop, „Den Gegner vernichten. Die Grenzsicherung der DDR", Bonn 1996, p. 100 and the road corssing points Friedrichstraße, Bornholmer Straße, Heinrich-Heine-Straße, Chausseestraße, Invalidenstraße, Oberbaumbrücke and Sonnenallee listed therein.

Road Border Crossings Berlin (West) — GDR	Sectors/Zone Crossing	Destination
Heiligensee/Stolpe-Dorf (since January 1, 1988)	French/ Soviet	Exchange and transit traffic by residents of Berlin (West) and the FRG as well as foreigners
Heerstraße/Staaken (until 31.12.1987)	British/ Soviet	Exchange and transit traffic by residents of Berlin (West) and the FRG as well as foreigners
Dreilinden/Drewitz Checkpoint Bravo	American/ Soviet	Exchange and transit traffic by residents of Berlin (West) and the FRG as well as foreigners
Kirchhainer Damm/Mahlow	American/ Soviet	Garbage transports from Berlin (West) into the GDR and transports of building materials from the GDR to Berlin (West)
Waltersdorfer Chaussee/Schönefeld	American/ Soviet	Exchange traffic by residents of Berlin (West) to the GDR-airport Berlin-Schönefeld, bus traffic, also transit traffic of persons and air cargo between the airport and Berlin (West)

S/U-Bahn and Long-Distance Traffic Border Crossing Station Berlin (East) — Berlin (West)	Sector Crossing	Destination
Friedrichstraße	Soviet/British	Exchange traffic of residents of Berlin (West) and the FRG as well as foreigners. Also exchange and transit traffic of persons in long-distance travel

Railway Crossing Points GDR — Berlin (West)	Zone/Sector Crossing	Destination
Staaken	Soviet/British	Transit traffic of persons, exchange and transit traffic of goods
Griebnitzsee	Soviet/American	Transit traffic of persons
Drewitz	Soviet/American	Exchange and transit traffic of goods

Water Border Crossing Points Berlin (East) — Berlin (West)	Sector Crossing	Destination
Marschallbrücke	Soviet/British	Exchange and transit traffic of goods, not from and to the FRG
Britzer Zweigkanal	Soviet/American	Exchange and transit traffic of goods, not from and to the FRG
Osthafen	Soviet/American	Exchange and transit traffic of goods, not from and to the FRG

Water Border Crossings GDR — Berlin (West)	Zone/Sectors Crossing	Destinations
Hennigsdorf	Soviet/French	Exchange and transit traffic of goods, not to and from the FRG
Nedlitz	Soviet/American	Exchange and transit traffic of goods
Babelsberger Enge	Soviet/American	Exchange traffic of goods
Dreilinden	Soviet/American	Exchange and transit traffic of goods
Kleinmachnow	Soviet/American	Exchange and transit traffic of goods

Additional Border Crossing Points[1] Fall 1989 until June 31, 1990 Berlin (West) — Berlin (Ost)	Sectors Crossing	Specifications
Kopenhagener Straße	French/Soviet	With and without car
Wollankstraße	French/Soviet	With and without car
Bernauer Straße/Eberswalder Straße	French/Soviet	Pedestrians only
Brunnenstraße	French/Soviet	Pedestrians only
U-Bahn station Rosenthaler Platz	Soviet/French	Pedestrians only
Brandenburger Tor	British/Soviet	Pedestrians only
Potsdamer Platz	British/Soviet	With and without car
Lindenstraße	American/Soviet	Pedestrians only
S-and U-Bahn station Jannowitzbrücke	Soviet/American	Pedestrians only
Köpenicker Straße/Schillingbrücke	American/Soviet	Pedestrians only
Schlesische Straße/Puschkinallee	American/Soviet	With and without car
Elsenstraße	American/Soviet	Pedestrians only
Stubenrauchstraße	American/Soviet	Pedestrians only

[1] Compiled according to "Berliner Stadtatlas", 16. edt., Berlin and others, 1990/91.

Additional Border Crossing Points[1] Fall 1989 until June 31, 1990 Berlin (West) — GDR	Sectors/Zone Crossing	Destinations
Berliner Straße	French/Soviet	Pedestrians only
Oranienburger Chaussee/ Hohen-Neuendorf	French/Soviet	Pedestrians only
Ruppiner Chaussee	French/Soviet	Pedestrians only
Falkenseer Chaussee/ Max-Reimann-Straße	British/Soviet	With or without car
Heerstraße/Staaken	British/Soviet	With or without car
Potsdamer Chaussee/ Groß Glienicke	British/Soviet	Pedestrians only (as of 1.6.1990 With or without car)
Glienicker Brücke	American/Soviet	With or without car
Böttcherberg	American/Soviet	Pedestrians only
Kohlhasenbrück	American/Soviet	Pedestrians only
Benschallee/Karl-Marx-Straße	American/Soviet	With or without car
Machnower Straße/ Zehlendorfer Damm	American/Soviet	With or without car
Teltower Damm/ Zehlendorfer Straße	American/Soviet	Pedestrians only
Ostpreußendamm/ Philipp-Müller-Allee	American/Soviet	With or without car
Marienfelder Allee	American/Soviet	Pedestrians only
Beethovenstraße/Mahlow	American/Soviet	Pedestrians only
Kirchhainer Damm/Mahlow	American/Soviet	With or without car
Groß Ziethener Straße	American/Soviet	Pedestrians only
Buckower Damm/Groß Ziethen	American/Soviet	Pedestrians only

[1] Compiled from "Berlin-Stadtatlas", l. c.

Border
crossing point
Prinzenstraße/
Heinrich-
Heine-Straße

Construction of the new wall near the Reichstag, July 1966

The Components of the Border Securing System at the Berlin Wall

Type of installation		Status: August 13, 1962[1]
Concrete wall with hollow blocks and barbed wire top	km	12
Barbed wire barrier	km	137
Used barbed wire	km	8 000–10 000
Iles, death and shooting strips	km²	450–500
Watchtowers[2] along the sector boundary	Number	32
Watchtowers along the border to the GDR	Number	84
Loudspeaker installations for the transmission of propaganda broadcasts to Berlin (West)	Number	216
Apartments compulsorily vacated in Bernauer Straße along the boundary of the districts of Wedding (French sector) and Mitte (Soviet sector) on September 24,1961 (appr.)	Number	580
Compulsorily evacuated residents of Bernauer Straße (appr.)	Number	2 000
Total length of bricked-up buildings in Bernauer Straße	km	0,75
Bricked-up building entrances in Bernauer Straße	Number	50
Bricked-up shops in Bernauer Straße	Number	37
Bricked-up windows Bernauer Straße	Number	1 253

[1] See „Verletzungen der Menschenrechte. Unrechtshandlungen und Zwischenfälle an der Berliner Sektorengrenze seit Errichtung der Mauer (13. August 1961–15. August 1962)", published upon commission of the federal government by the Federal Ministry for All-German Questions, Bonn and Berlin [1962], p. 17f.
[2] The watchtowers were up to 20 m high and normally equipped with searchlights and a telephone connection, staffed day and night with double guards. See „Ulbrichts Mauer", l. c., p. 10.

Type of Installation		Status: 1971[1]	Status: 1981[2]
Concrete slab wall with and without pipe top[3]	km	99.8	107.0
Metal lattice fence	km	53.8	55.4
Barbed wire blockade	km	8.5	4.8
Concrete wall, remainders of facades, property walls	km	11.6	9.0
Observation towers, stands[4]	Number	243	287
Bunkers	Number	144	137
Dog installations	Number	221	275
Car blocking trenches	km	106.2	108.0
Contact, signal fence	km	120.0	123.5
Convoy paths (concreted)	km	122.7	123.5
Use of firearms by border defence forces	Occasions	1 360	1 591
Projectile strikes in Berlin (West) with damage to persons	Projectiles	20	20
with damage to property	Projectiles	356	436
Use of firearms by the police force	Occasions	14	14
Tear gas launches by the border defence forces	Occasions	428	428
Tear gas launches by the police force	Occasions	125	126
Arrests at the wall that became public	Persons	2 838	3 097

[1] See „13. August 1961 — 13. August 1971, Dokumentation Berlin", published by the Press and Information Office of the State of Berlin, Berlin 1971, p. 9.

[2] See H. Pastor, „Die Mauer heute", Berlin 1982.

[3] As of 1965, the wall was extended to become the so-called „modern border" by means of the step-by-step replacement of the bricked wall sections with app. 3.5 m high concrete slabs set between steel girders, the top consisting of a pipe with a diameter of approximately 35 cm. See "Berlin Handbuch", l. c., p. 807f.
As of 1976, erection of the so-called Border Wall 75" in stages: L-shaped 3.60 m respectively 2.40 m high, seamless concrete segments with a strength of 15 cm and a width of 1.20 m placed 2.10 m deep into the ground with a base in the shape of a abutment and a top consisting of a asbestos pipe with a diameter of 40 cm. See Th. Flemming and H. Koch, „Die Berliner Mauer. Geschichte eines politischen Bauwerks", Berlin 1999, p. 82 pp.

[4] As of 1966, erection of mushroom-shaped observation towers (BT-11), as of 1975 angular observation towers (BT-9). See Lapp, „Gefechtsdienst im Frieden", l. c., p. 245 and Ritter, Lapp, „Die Grenze", l. c., p. 110.

Type of Installation		Status: July 31[1]					
		1984	1985	1986	1987	1988	1989
Concrete slab wall	km	112.6	111.6	111.2	107.6	107.0	106.0
Metal lattice fence	km	55.0	55.7	58.4	62.3	61.3	66.5
Barbed wire	km	4.8					
Concrete wall, remainders of facades, property walls	km	9.0	0.5[2]	0.5	0.5	0.5	0.5
Observation towers	km	285	293	299	296	296	302
Bunkers	Number	69	52	43	30	24	20
Dog installations	Number	256	258	244	250	255	259
Car blocking trenches	km	108.0	108.0	107.3	106.2	105.5	105.5
Contact, signal fence	km	124.9	124.9	125.1	125.3	127.5	127.5
Convoy path	km	123.5	124.0	124.0	124.0	124.0	124.3

[1] Source: The Chief of Police of Berlin, here quoted from: Ritter, Lapp, „Die Grenze", l. c., p. 166.

[2] Property walls on the plot of Bergmann Borsig Company in Berlin-Pankow.

Border soldiers
guarding the
construction
of the wall, here
still without the
barbed wire top

The Organisation of the Border Regime

Border soldier guarding the construction of the wall in Zimmerstraße, Berlin-Mitte, August 1961

Border fortification work in the Hochröhn

Safeguarding measures after an escape attempt

The Organisation of the Border Police/Troops of the SOZ/GDR

Superior Authority	Name	Periods of subordination[1]
German Interior Administration[2]	German Border Police[3]	1946–1949
Main Administration of the German People's Police in the Ministry of the Interior	German Border Police	1949–1952
Ministry of National Security	German Border Police	1952–1953
Ministry of National Security	German Border Police	1953–1955
State Secretariat for National Security	German Border Police	1955
Ministry of National Security	German Border Police	1955–1957
Ministry of the Interior	German Border Police	1957–1961
Ministry of National Defence	Border Commando of the National People's Army	1961–1973
Ministry of National Defence	GDR Border Troops	1974–1989
Ministry of Disarmament and National Defence	GDR Border Troops	1990

In the state of	until	Achieved Force Level of the Border Police[4]
Mecklenburg	30.11.1946	375
Brandenburg	26.11.1946	205
Saxony-Anhalt	23.11.1946	300
Saxony	27.11.1946	771
Thuringia	01.12.1946	874

[1] See „DDR-Handbuch", volume 1, published by the Federal Ministry of Inner-German relations, 3rd revised and augmented edition, Cologne 1985, p. 575 pp. and Lapp, "Gefechtsdienst im Frieden", l. c., p. 233–239.

[2] Central Administration of the Interior, established upon order of the Soviet military administration of June 30, 1946 with the main duty of police organisation and the education of suitable new recruits for the German police forces reinforced and unified in 1946 in the Soviet occupied zone (SOZ). See D. M. Schneider, „Innere Verwaltung/Deutsche Verwaltung des Innern (DVdI)", in: M. Broszat and H. Weber (publishers), SOZ-manual. National administrations, parties, social organisations and their executives in the Soviet occupied zone in Germany 1945–1949, 2nd edition, Munich 1993, p. 211.

[3] Special police forces established upon order of the Soviet military administration of November 18, 1946 and their official order of December 12, 1946, initially on state level, since 1948 directly subordinated, quartered and educated militarily by the German Administration of the Interior. See Schneider, „Innere Verwaltung/Deutsche Verwaltung des Innern", l. c., p. 213p. and D. Schultke, „Keiner kommt durch. Die Geschichte der innerdeutschen Grenze 1945–1990", Berlin 1999, p. 19.

[4] See Schultke, „Keiner kommt durch", l. c., p. 18 f.

Year	Strength of the Border Police/Troops in Persons (app.)[1]
1946	2 500
1947	4 000
1948	10 000
1949	18 000
1950	20 000
1951	20 000
1952	20 000
1953	25 500
1954	31 000
1958	35 000
1960	38 000
1961	38 000
1962	52 000
1963	52 000

Armament/Equipment of the Border Police at the Time it was Placed under the Charge of the Ministry of National Defense in 1961	Units[2]
Medium-sized tanks	60
Floating amoured wagons	373
Small arms	39 391
Light machine guns	2 813
40 mm Panzerbüchsen	2 784
82 mm recoil-free guns	220
107 mm recoil-free guns	54
85 mm self-firing canons	144
Motorcycles	794
Cars and special vehicles	1 221
Trucks	1 365
Coastal and port protection boats	2 035

Category of Draftees in the GDR	Judgement of the Wehrkreiskommando[3]
With contact to 1st and 2nd degree relatives in the FRG	Unsuited for border duty
Without contact to 1st and 2nd degree relatives in the FRG	Suited for border duty

[1] Statements according to Lapp, „Frontdienst im Frieden", l. c., „Gefechtsdienst im Frieden", l. c., and Schultke, „Keiner kommt durch", l. c. Strength of the boder troops from the beginning of the seventies until the downfall of the GDR: app. 50 000 men — see there.
[2] See Schultke, „Keiner kommt durch", l. c., p. 67.
[3] Source: Federal Border Police; here quoted according to: Schultke, „Keiner kommt durch", l. c., p. 100.

Categories of Border Soldiers in the GDR	Assessment by the Officers of the Border Troops[1]
Category A	Can be deployed with any member of the border troops beyond the last blocking facility and up to the border pillars.
Category B	Can be deployed up to the last convoy path or with an „A-classified" in the entire border area.
Category B 1	Can be deployed with an „A-classified" in the entire border area or with a „B-classified" up to the first convoy path.
Category B 2	Deployable like category B 1 with slight reduction of reliability.
Category C	Soldier on leave and all posted soldiers.
Category D 1	Can only be deployed with an „A-classified" and only up to the first blocking installations.
Category D 2	Can only be entrusted with maintenance work within the border company or deployed as guard within the barracks.

Distribution of SED-members within the border troops	1961 in %[2]
Officers	33.7
NCOs	32.7
Soldiers	33.6

SED-members in the border troops	1987/1988 in %[3]
Officers	96.9
Ensigns	97.3
Regular NCOs	74.1
NCOs serving for a fixed period in the 1st year of training	21.7
Soldiers in their 18-month basic military service	7.9

Social origin of the border troops	1988 in %[4]
Workers	88.8
Members of agricultural collectives	6.8
Employees	1.7
Students	0.9
Intelligence	0.7
Members of a crafts collective	0.7
Self-employed craftsmen	0.1
Others	0.3

[1] Source: Federal Border Police. Here quoted from: Schultke, „Keiner kommt durch", l. c., p. 101.
[2] On the target date September 30, 1961 12 064 soldiers of 38 318 were members or candidates of the SED — see Koop, „Den Gegner vernichten",l. c., p. 113. Please note: voluntary military service in the GDR until the passing of the Military Service Law of January 24, 1962.
[3] Source: files of the former GDR border troops in the military archive of the Federal Archive in Freiburg. Here quoted from: Ritter, Lapp, „Die Grenze", l. c., p. 97 pp.
[4] Source: files of the former GDR border troops in the military archive of the Federal Archive in Freiburg. Here quoted from: Schultke, „Keiner kommt durch", l. c., p. 102.

Cons. no.	Legal Norm: Border Protection	Date[1]
1	Order about the measures along the demarcation line between the GDR and the western occupied zones in Germany (GBl., p. 405)	26.05.1952
2	Police order (by the Ministry of National Security) about the introduction of a special order along the demarcation line (announcement)	26.05.1952
3	Order about further measures for the protection of the GDR (GBl., p. 451)	09.06.1952
4	Order about the regulation of the interzonal traffic (GBl., p. 1157)	21.11.1953
5	Decree about the new regulation of the measures along the demarcation line between the GDR and West Germany (central gazette of the Ministry of the Interior of the GDR of 26.6.1954, p. 266f.)	18.06.1954
6	Order about the alleviation and regulation of measures along the border between the GDR and the Federal Republic of Germany (GBl. I, p. 385)	03.05.1956
7	Order for the guarantee of security long the western border of the GDR (announcement)	21.09.1961
8	Order about the securing and the protection of the coastal areas of the GDR (GBl. II, p. 409)	21.06.1962
9	Decree about measures for securing the coastal areas of the GDR (GBl. II, p. 410)	10.07.1962
10	Order about measures for the protection of the national border between the GDR and West Berlin (GBl. II, p. 381)	21.06.1963
11	Order about the erection of a frontier zone along the national border between the GDR and West Berlin (GBl. III, p. 382)	21.06.1963
12	Instructions about the order in the frontier zone along the national border between the GDR and West Berlin (GBl. II, p. 382)	21.06.1963
13	Decree for the protection of the national border of the GDR (GBl. II, p. 255)	19.03.1964
14	Instructions about the order in the frontier zones and territorial waters of the GDR (border regulation) (GBl. II, p. 257)	19.03.1964
15	Instructions about the order in the frontier zones and territorial waters of the GDR (border regulation) (GBl. II, p. 483)	15.06.1972
16	Law governing the national border of the GDR (GBl. I, p. 197)	25.03.1982
17	Implementing order for the law governing the national border of the GDR (GBl. I, p. 203)	25.03.1982
18	Decree about the order in the frontier zones and the lakes of the GDR (border regulation) (GBl. I, p. 208)	25.03.1982

[1] See Lapp, „Gefechtsdienst im Frieden", l. c., p. 232 pp.

No.	Legal Norm: Use of Firearms	Regulation	Date[1]
1	Guidelines for the agencies of the German police for the protection of the demarcation line in the SOZ Germany of the Commander-in Chief of the Soviet occupational forces and main authorized representative of the SMAD, Marshall W.Sokolowskij, § 20 lit. b	In the following cases, border units and members of the border police may result to the use of firearms: ... escapes by border violators and violators of the demarcation line, if other possibilities of arrest are exhausted (warnings, shots in the air) ...	23.08. 1947
2	Police decree (by the Ministry of National Security) about the introduction of a special order along the demarcation line, § 4	The crossing of the 10 m control strip is prohibited for all persons... In case of non-compliance of the orders of the border police, firearms will be used.	26.05. 1952
3	Guidelines for the regulations concerning the use of firearms by the armed organs of the German Democratic Republic by the Security Commission of the SED politburo, confirmed in the subsequent session of the SED politburo.	The use of firearms along the national border West and North (Sea), the circle around Berlin and at the Berlin sector boundaries is prohibited except in cases of self-defence against armed attacks. The necessary measures against illegal border crossers or persons and vehicles that try to avoid control through escape directly at the border have to be executed with other qualified means.	22.1. 1959/ 24.2. 1959
4	Order no. 39/60 by the Ministry of the Interior: use of firearms in case of border violations	Firearms ... may ... be used ....when arresting spies, saboteurs, provocateurs and other criminals if they put up armed resistance against their arrest or attempt to escape...	28.06. 1960
5	Order no. 76/61 by the Ministry of National Defence: Regulations regarding the use of firearms for the border commando of the National People's Army	Order to the border patrols on the inner-German border, „to use firearms in the following cases: ... For the arrest of persons that do not adhere to the instructions of the border patrols and do not stop after the order ‚Stop – Freeze – Border Patrol or after the firing of a warning shot but instead try to violate the national border of the GDR....“	06.10. 1961
6	Implementing order no. 2 relating to order no. 39/60 of the Ministry of the Interior	Obligation of the border patrol around Berlin „to use firearms in the following cases: ... For the arrest of persons that do not adhere to the instructions of the border patrols and do not stop after the order ‚Stop – Freeze – Border Patrol or after the firing of a warning shot but instead try to violate the national border of the GDR....“	19.03. 1962[2]
7	Law about the duties and authorities of the German People's Police, § 17 II p. 1 (GBl. I, p. 237)	The use of firearms is justified in order to prevent the imminent commitment or continuation of an offence whose circumstances constitute a crime.[3]	11.06. 1968
8	Border law, § 27 II p. 1 (GBl. I, p. 197)	The use of firearms is justified in order to prevent the imminent commitment or continuation of an offence whose circumstances constitute a crime.	25.03. 1982

[1] Selection, compiled after H. Rosenau, „Tödliche Schüsse im staatlichen Auftrag. Die strafrechtliche Verantwortung von Grenzsoldaten für den Schußwaffengebrauch an der deutsch-deutschen Grenze“, 2nd revised edition, Baden-Baden 1998, p. 42–80; here one also finds references to excerpts of regulations concerning the use of firearms in Koop, „Den Gegner vernichten“, l. c.

[2] Regulation of the use of firearms in the follow-up time through numerous service regulations and an annual so-called „Order 101“ by the Ministry of National Defense, here omitted.

[3] Please note the criminal nature of the so-called „illegal border crossing“ according to § 213 StGB-DDR of 12.1.1968 (GBl. I, p. 1).

Use of Firearms for the Prevention of Illegal Border Crossings[1]

Cons. no.	Date	Time	Unit	Reason	Place	No. of shots	Arrest	Crossing	Injured	Killed
1	15.12.1968	01.05 am	4./37	Att. BR[2]	Wredebrücke[3]	2	X			
2	24.12.1969	9.04 pm	2./33	Att. BC[4]	HdM/VdK[5]	5	X			
3	13.01.1969	5.50 pm	2./33	Att. BC	Kronprinzenbrücke[6]	2	X			
4	28.01.1969	8.50 pm	3./31	Att. BC	Eberswalder Str.[7]	80	X			
5	03.02.1969	01.28 am	3./37	Border cross.	Massantebrücke[8]	48		X		
6	03.02.1969	6.55 pm	2./33	Att. BC	Voßstraße[9]	12	X			
7	09.04.1969	9.50 pm	1./35	Att. BC	Adalbertstraße[10]	148	X			X[11]
8	11.04.1969	03.05 am	2./38	Att. BC	Potsdamer Pl.[12]	45	X		X	
9	06.06.1969	00.34 am	3./38	Border cross.	Adalbertstraße	61		X		
10	13.06.1969	02.55 am	3./33	Att. BC	HdM/O.-Gr.-Str.[13]	22	X			
					11 persons	425	8	2	1	1

[1] Source: Investigative report of the 1st Border Brigade of the National People's Army of the GDR of June 17, 1969, classified information no. H 32 158, p. 6; here quoted from: Koop, „Den Gegner vernichten", l. c., p. 126.

[2] BR: Border regulation.

[3] Wredebrücke across Teltowkanal from Rudower Chaussee in the East Berlin district of Treptow to Köpenicker Straße in the West Berlin district of Neukölln.

[4] Att. BC: Attempted border crossing

[5] HdM: House of Ministries, former Air Ministry of the Third Reich, today Detlev-Rohwedder-House, in Leipziger Straße in the Berlin district of Mitte; VdK: Association of German Consumer Cooperatives.

[6] Kronprinzenbrücke across the Spree from Reinhardtstraße in the East Berlin district of Mitte to Fürst-Bismarck-Straße in the West Berlin district of Tiergarten.

[7] Eberswalder Straße in the East Berlin district of Prenzlauer Berg, extension: Bernauer Straße in the West Berlin district of Wedding.

[8] Massantebrücke across Teltowkanal/Stubenrauchstraße from the East Berlin disctict of Treptow into the West Berlin district of Neukölln.

[9] Voßstraße in the East Berlin disctict of Mitte near Potsdamer Platz.

[10] Adalbertstraße across the sector boundary from the East Berlin district of Mitte to the West Berlin district of Kreuzberg.

[11] Johannes Lange (1940–1969); see 126th press conference of the Work Group August 13 of August 11 2000 in the House at Checkpoint Charlie, Berlin, p. 18.

[12] Potsdamer Platz in the East Berlin district of Mitte.

[13] Otto-Grotewohl-Straße, formerly and again today Wilhelmstraße in the East-Berlin district of Mitte.

Escape through
the barbed wire
fence, 1961

The German-German
Escape Movement

Refugee camp
Berlin-Neukölln,
Siegfriedstraße,
March 1953

Transit camp Berlin-Marienfelde, 1960/1961

August 15, 1961, Bernauer Straße: the first escaped border soldier, Conrad Schumann

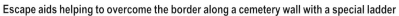

Escape aids helping to overcome the border along a cemetery wall with a special ladder

Migrants GDR — FRG 1949–1961[1]

Year	Number without permission (escapees)	Without permission (escapees) in %	Number with permission (legal emigrants)	With permission (legal emigrants) in %	Total	Via Berlin (West)[2]	Via other Eastern Block states[3]	Blockade breakers[4]	Smugglers[5]
1949	129 245	100.0			129 245				
1950	197 788	100.0			197 788				
1951	165 648	100.0			165 648	193 227[6]			
1952	182 393	100.0			182 393	118 300			
1953	331 390	100.0			331 390	305 737			
1954	184 198	100.0			184 198	104 399			
1955	252 870	100.0			252 870	153 693			
1956	279 189	100.0			279 189	156 377			
1957	261 622	100.0			261 622	129 579			
1958	204 092	100.0			204 092	119 552			
1959	143 917	100.0			143 917	90 862			
1960	199 188	100.0			199 188	152 291			
Until 12.8.61	155 402	100.0			155 402	125 053			

[1] Source: Federal Compensation Office; here quoted from: H. Wendt, „Die deutsch-deutschen Wanderungen — Bilanz einer 40jährigen Geschichte von Flucht und Ausreise", in: Deutschland Archiv 24 (1991) 4, p. 390.
Definition of migrants: all migrants between the GDR and the FRG, meaning including all escapees, escapees via third-party states or blockage breakers, retirees or persons reunited with their families, persons who legally came to the FRG because of family celebrations or occupiers of the embassy in 1989, all in all all persons that left the GDR from November 1989 until June 1990 — see there, page 387.

[2] See „Die Mauer und ihr Fall", l. c., p. 24.

[3] See M. Tantzscher, „Die verlängerte Mauer. Die Zusammenarbeit der Sicherheitsdienste der Warschauer-Pakt-Staaten bei der Verhinderung von „Republikflucht", Berlin 1998 (= BStU, series B: Analyses and Reports No. 1/1998), p. 77.

[4] Crossing the border fortifications under danger of death, stated figures see Ritter, Lapp, „Die Grenze", l. c., p. 167.

[5] See Tantzscher, „Die verlängerte Mauer", l. c., p. 77.

[6] 1949–1951.

Migrants GDR — FRG 1961–1990[1]

Year	Number without permission (escapees)	Without permission (escapees) in %	Number with permission (legal emigrants)	With permission (legal emigrants) in %	Total	Via Berlin (West)[2]	Via other Eastern Block states[3]	Blockade breakers[4]	Smuggles[5]
Since 13.8.61	51 624	100.0			51 624			8 507[6]	
1962	16 741	78.4	4 624	21.6	21 365			5 761	
1963	12 967	30.4	29 665	69.6	42 632			3 692	
1964	11 864	28.3	30 012	71.7	41 876			3 155	
1965	11 886	40.2	17 666	59.8	29 552			2 329	
1966	8 456	35.0	15 675	65.0	24 131			1 736	
1967	6 385	32.6	13 188	67.4	19 573			1 203	
1968	4 902	30.6	11 134	69.4	16 036			1 135	
1969	5 273	31.1	11 702	68.9	16 975			1 193	
1970	5 047	28.8	12 472	71.2	17 519			901	
1971	5 843	33.6	11 565	66.4	17 408			832	
1972	5 537	32.3	11 627	67.7	17 164		147	1 245	308
1973	6 522	42.9	8 667	57.1	15 189		203	1 842	953
1974	5 324	40.2	7 928	59.8	13 252		116	969	433
1975	6 011	36.9	10 274	63.1	16 285		88	673	305
1976	5 110	33.7	10 058	66.3	15 168		87	610	287
1977	4 037	33.4	8 041	66.6	12 078		111	721	215
1978	3 846	31.7	8 271	68.3	12 117		113	461	118
1979	3 512	28.1	9 003	71.9	12 515		161	463	86
1980	3 988	31.2	8 775	68.8	12 763		136	424	72
1981	4 340	28.1	11 093	71.9	15 433		119	298	129
1982	4 095	31.0	9 113	69.0	13 208		121	283	89
1983	3 614	31.9	7 729	68.1	11 343		130	228	85
1984	5 992	14.6	34 982	85.4	40 974		67	192	39
1985	6 160	24.7	18 752	75.3	24 912		86	160	29
1986	6 196	23.7	19 982	76.3	26 178			210	32
1987	7 499	39.6	11 459	60.4	18 958		133	288	47
1988	11 893	29.9	27 939	70.1	39 832		319	590	68
1989	241 907	70.4	101 947	29.6	343 854				
Until 30.6.90					238 384				

[1] Source: Federal Compensation Office; here quoted from: Wendt, „Die deutsch-deutschen Wanderungen", l. c., p. 390.
[2] See „Die Mauer und ihr Fall", l. c., p. 24.
[3] See Tantzscher, „Die verlängerte Mauer", l. c., p. 77.
[4] Crossing the border fortifications under danger of death, stated figures see Ritter, Lapp, „Die Grenze", l. c., p. 167.
[5] See Tantzscher, „Die verlängerte Mauer", l. c., p. 77.
[6] 1.1.1961–31.12.1961.

1953	Number of Migrants GDR – FRG[1]
January	22 396
February	31 613
March	58 605
April	36 695
May	35 484
June	40 381
July	17 260
August	14 682
September	19 267
October	22 032
November	19 913
December	13 062

1961	Number of Migrants GDR – FRG[2]
January	16 697
February	13 576
March	16 094
April	19 803
May	17 791
June	19 198
July	30 415
August	47 433
September	14 821
October	5 366
November	3 412
December	2 420

[1] See „Die Flucht aus der Sowjetzone und die Sperrmaßnahmen des kommunistischen Regimes vom 13. August 1961 in Berlin", published by the Federal Ministry for All-German Questions, 2nd revised edition, Bonn and Berlin 1961, diagram.

[2] Source: Federal Ministry for Expellees, Refugees and Persons Injured through War; here quoted from: J. Rühle and G. Holzweißig, August 13, 1961. "Die Mauer von Berlin", 2nd augmented edition, Cologne 1986 (= Edition German Archive), p. 154.

Migrants GDR – FRG January 1989 – June 1990[1]

Month/Year	Without permission (refugees) number	Without permission (refugees) in %	With permission (legal departures) number	With permission (legal departures) in %	Total
1989					
January	886	19.1	3 741	80.9	4 627
February	921	18.4	4 087	81.6	5 008
March	1 184	20.9	4 487	79.1	5 671
April	891	15.1	4 996	84.9	5 887
May	1 527	14.3	9 115	85.7	10 642
June	1 783	14.3	10 645	85.7	12 428
July	2 144	18.3	9 563	81.7	11 707
August	8 143	38.9	12 812	61.1	20 955
September	21 352	64.2	11 903	35.8	33 255
October	26 426	46.3	30 598	53.7	57 024
November					133 429
December					43 221
Total					343 854
Jan.-Oct.	65 257	39.0	101 947	61.0	167 204
1990					
January					73 729
February					63 893
March					46 241
April					24 615
May					19 217
June					10 689
Jan.-June					238 384

[1] Source: Federal Compensation Office; here quoted from: Wendt, „Die deutsch-deutschen Wanderungen", l. c., p. 393.

Inner-German Migrations according to Time Periods[1]

Time Period	Migrations from the GDR to the FRG			Emigrations into the GDR	Migration balance
	Total	of those refugees[2]	Refugees in %		
1950–1961	3 854 552	2 609 321	67.7	400 315	3 454 237
1950–1988	4 480 303	3 173 757	70.8	470 252	4 010 051
1950–1989	4 868 699	3 517 611	72.2	471 381	4 397 318
1950–1990[3]	5 107 083	3 755 995	73.5		
1962–1969	221 538	140 712	63.5	37 209	184 329
1962–1988	625 751	564 436	90.2	69 937	555 814
1962–1989	1 014 147	908 290	93.7	75 072	939 075
1970–1979	174 876	148 695	85.0	15 344	159 532
1980–1988	229 337	203 601	88.8	17 384	211 953

[1] Source: Federal Statistics Office, Federal Compensation Office; here quoted from: Wendt, „Die deutsch-deutschen Wanderungen", l. c., p. 388.
[2] Migrants registered as refugees.
[3] Until June 1990.

Migrants divided into Age Groups in %[1]

Year	under 25	25–65	65 and over
1955	52.5	43.5	4.0
1965	10.4	38.1	51.5
1974	15.1	45.6	39.3
1985	34.9	52.5	12.6
1989	45.7	51.3	3.0

[1] Source: Federal Statistics Office; here quoted from: Wendt, „Die deutsch-deutschen Wanderungen", l. c., p. 391.

Share of Occupational Groups
in the Total of Escapees[1]

Occupational group	(1952/62)
Cultivation and animal breeding	155 461
Industry and crafts	470 080
Technical professions	47 561
Trade and traffic	268 082
Household, health services, etc.	113 500
Administration and legal system	71 595
Spiritual and artistic life	38 467
Undefined professions	234 285
Employees	1 399 631
Pensioners and retirees	131 724
Housewives	257 261
Children and pupils	466 074
Students	15 079
Total	2 269 769
Intelligent professions	(1954/62)
Doctors	3 948
Dentists	1 495
Veterinaries	344
Druggists	1 018
Judges and public prosecutors	194
Lawyers and notaries	704
University teachers	775
Other teachers	17 995
Engineers and technicians	19 102

[1] See „A–Z. Ein Taschen- und Nachschlagebuch über den anderen Teil Deutschlands", published by the Federal Ministry for All-German Questions, 11th edition, Bonn 1969, p. 213.

Escapes of Border Policemen / Soldiers until July 31, 1989[1]

Year	Number	Year	Number
1961	285	1976	6
1962	455	1977	10
1963	317	1978	6
1964	134	1979	6
1965	194	1980	9
1966	158	1981	15
1967	112	1982	16
1968	54	1983	14
1969	73	1984	11
1970	57	1985	10
1971	54	1986	16
1972	33	1987	21
1973	28	1988	14
1974	22	1989	14
1975	12		

[1] See „Menschenrechte in der DDR und Berlin (Ost)", published by the International Association for Human Rights — German Chapter —, Frankfurt a. M., work committee „Civil Rights Movement and Political Prisoners in the GDR", 3rd edition, Frankfurt a. M. 1988, p. 70; also 90th press conference of the work group August 13 of August 11, 1989 in their House at Checkpoint Charlie, Berlin, p. 13; here quoted from Lapp, "Gefechtsdienst im Frieden", l. c., p. 93.

Desertions, Illegal Border Crossings and Migrations by Collaborators and former Collaborators of the Ministry of National Security (MfS)[1]

	1950–1960	1961–1970	1971–1980	1981–1988	Total
Desertions and illegal border crossings by collaborators (of those operative collaborators[2])	92 (51)	17 (11)	2 (2)	0	111 (64)
Illegal border crossings by former collaborators (of those operative collaborators)	308 (57)	54 (54)	5 (1)	6 (k. A.)	373 (68)
Total	400 (108)	71 (21)	7 (3)	6 (k. A.)	484 (132)
of those „back"	108	12	1	k. A.	120
of those sentenced to death	7	-	-	k. A.	7
Releases/migrations of former collaborators to the FRG	1	3	3	105	112

[1] See J. Gieseke, „Die hauptamtlichen Mitarbeiter des Ministeriums für Staatssicherheit", 2nd edition, Berlin 1996 (= MfS-manual, vol. IV/1), p. 81.
[2] Operative collaborators = operative forces: total of the official and unofficial collaborators deployed for the solving of political and operative tasks of the Ministry of National Security (MfS).
Political and operative tasks: the activities of the operative collaborators of the MfS for the realisation of the security requirements of the socialist society based on the class assignment of the SED; see S. Suckut (publisher), "Das Wörterbuch der Staatssicherheit. Definitionen zur „politisch-operativen Arbeit", Berlin 1996 (= scientific series of the BStU, vol. 5), p. 52 and p. 265.

Escapes by Tunnel[1]

Location of the Escape Tunnel to Berlin (West)	Discovery	Result
Tunnel in the north of Berlin	1961/1962	Successfully used by 28 escapees
Gleim tunnel	1961/1962	Successfully used
Bahnhofstraße	21.12.1961	Successfully used
Oranienburger Chaussee 13	24.01.1962	Successfully used by 26 escapees
Wollankstraße	27.01.1962	Discovered prior to use
Kleinmachnow[2]	07.02.1962	Discovered prior to use
Dresdener Straße 34/35	27.03.1962	Discovered prior to use
Heidelberger Straße 35	27.03.1962	Successfully used; Death of the West Berlin tunnel digger Heinz Jercha
Harzer Straße	April 1962	Discovered prior to use
Oranienburger Chaussee 22	05.05.1962	Successfully used by 12 escapees
Elsenstraße 85	12.06.1962	Discovered, use not known
VEB Bergmann Borsig	12.06.1962	Successfully used by 3 escapees
Zimmerstraße 56	18.06.1962	Successfully used by 4 escapees; Death of the GDR border soldier Reinhold Huhn
Sebastianstraße 81	28.06.1962	Death of the West Berlin tunnel digger Siegfried Noffke
Heidelberger Straße 75	29.06.1962	Discovered prior to use
Schwedter Straße	02.07.1962	Successfully used by at least 5 escapees
Schützen-/Bahnhofstraße	09.07.1962	Discovered; use not known
Melchiorstraße	July 1962	Discovered; use not known
Elsenstraße 41	July 1962	Discovered; use not known
Puderstraße 7	07./08.08.1962	Discovered prior to use
Bernauer Straße	September 1962	Successfully used by 29 escapees
Glienicke	March 1963	Successfully used by 16 escapees
Kremmener Straße	23.05.1963	Discovered prior to use
Bernauer Straße	05.10.1964	Successfully used by 57 escapees. Death of the GDR border soldier Egon Schultz
Zimmerstraße	1971/1972	Successfully used

[1] Source: Work Group 13 August. List incomplete — additional indications of escapes by tunnel can possibly be found in the archives of BStU and BArch-SAPMO.
[2] Community that borders the West Berlin district of Zehlendorf in the southwest.

Escapes across the Baltic Sea[1]

Year	Failed border crossings:		Successful border crossings:			
	Arrests	Deaths	Information of GDR Border Brigade Coast (GBK)	Information of FRG Border Police (BGS)	Information GBK Total	Information GBK/BGS Total
13.8.–31.12.1961	69		30		99	
1962	n/a	3				
1963	168	–	9		177	
1964	247	2	99		348	
1964/65	177	2	29		208	
1965/66	210	2	33		245	
1966/67	137	1	23		161	
1967/68	88	–	11		99	
1968/69	123	1	24		148	
1969/End of 1970	161	1	26	44	187	206
1971	215	2	19	51	236	268
1972	228	–	20	52	248	280
1973	229	1	14	33	244	263
1974	100	2	23	35	125	137
1975	109	–	11	33	120	142
1976	158	–	20	28	178	186
1977	253	3	16	38	272	294
1978	129	–	11	20	140	149
1979	154	3	10	20	167	177
1979/80	153	–	5	18	158	171
1980/81	152	–	21	42	173	194
1981/82	172	–	10	10	182	182
1982/83	155	1	5	6	161	162
1983/84	115	–	7	12	122	127
1984/85	87	1	1	5	89	93
1985/86	78	–	4	10	82	88
1986/87	115	–	10	15	125	130
1987/88	173	1	27	36	226	236
1.1.–9.11.1989	117	1	73	32	191	150
Total	4 272	27	591	594	4 914	3 635

[1] See C. and B. Müller, „Über die Ostsee in die Freiheit. Dramatische Fluchtgeschichten", 2nd edition, Bielefeld 1992, p. 52.

Prevented Escape Attempts[1]

Year	Total	Of those via other Eastern Block states	Of those smuggled out
1971	3 263	n/a	39
1972	3 835	n/a	73
1973	3 945	n/a	237
1974	3 497	n/a	294
1975	2 566	1 793	141
1976	3 620	1 517	191
1977	3 601	1 333	233
1978	2 886	1 181	254
1979	2 856	1 162	259
1980	3 321	1 411	315
1981	2 912	1 261	211
1982	3 077	1 406	131
1983	2 910	1 331	100
1984	1 968	835	59
1985	1 509	827	61
1986	2 173	882	34
1987	3 006	1 211	35
1988	4 224	1 768	81

[1] See Tantzscher, „Die verlängerte Mauer", l. c., p. 77.

Relief and joy after a successful tunnel escape, 1963/1964

Two East Berliners are taken away after a failed escape attempt.
Berlin, Dresdener Straße, August 1962

Border crossing point Herleshausen, ransomed prisoners from GDR-prisons are brought to West Germany under strict observance of secrecy, September 1977

Rush of GDR-citizens wanting to leave the GDR on the embassy of the Federal Republic of Germany, fall 1989

Ransomed Prisoners[1]

Year	Number	Year	Number
1963	8	1977	1 475
1964	888	1978	1 452
1965	1 541	1979	890
1966	424	1980	1 036
1967	531	1981	1 584
1968	696	1982	1 491
1969	927	1983	1 105
1970	888	1984	2 236
1971	1 375	1985	2 669
1972	731	1986	1 450
1973	631	1987	1 209
1974	1 053	1988	1 048
1975	1 158	1989	1 840
1976	1 439	Total	31 775

[1] Source concerning the release of political prisoners in the GDR in the scope of the special attempts on behalf of the federal government: Ministry of the Interior, Principal of the Ministry K. Plewa; here quoted from: "Im Namen des Volkes. Über die Justiz im Staat der SED". Catalogue of the exhibition by the Ministry of Justice, published by the Ministry of Justice, 2nd edition, Leipzig 1996, p. 232.

Income of the GDR from the Ransoming of Political Prisoners through the FRG[1]

Year	DM in million	Year	DM in million
1964	37.9	1976	130.0
1965	67.6	1977	143.9
1966	24.8	1978	168.3
1967	31.4	1979	106.9
1968	28.4	1980	130.0
1969	44.8	1981	178.0
1970	50.6	1982	176.9
1971	84.2	1983	102.8
1972	69.4	1984	387.9
1973	54.0	1985	302.0
1974	88.1	Total	2 511.9[2]
1975	104,0		

[1] Source: Analysis about special business „B" of A. Schalck-Golodkowski; here quoted from: P. Przybylski, "Tatort Politbüro. Die Akte Honecker", Berlin 1991, p. 367.
[2] Total income of the GDR from the ransoming of prisoners by the FRG from 1963–1989: over 3.5 billion DM; see L. A. Rehlinger, "Freikauf. Die Geschäfte der DDR mit politisch Verfolgten 1963–1989", Berlin and Frankfurt a. M. 1991, p. 247.

Time period	Costs per head for the ransoming of prisoners in DM[1]
1963–1976	app. 40 000
1977–1989	app. 96 000

[1] See W. Weidenfeld and K.-R. Korte (publishers), „Handbuch zur deutschen Einheit 1949–1989–1999", Bonn 1999 (= series of publications by the Central Federal Office for Political Education, volume 363), p. 447.

West-East-Migrations from the FRG to the GDR from 1950–1968[1]

Year	Total absolute	Number of repatriates	Repatriates in %	Number of settlers[2]	Settlers in %
1950	27 543	n/a[3]	n/a	n/a	n/a
1951	24 880	n/a	n/a	n/a	n/a
1952	23 134	n/a	n/a	n/a	n/a
1953	31 792	n/a	n/a	n/a	n/a
1954	75 867	41 999	55.4	33 868	44.6
1955	72 922	41 937	57.5	30 985	42.5
1956	73 868	48 625	65.8	25 243	34.2
1957	77 924	58 247	74.7	19 677	25.3
1958	55 500	43 103	78.9	12 397	22.7
1959	63 083	41 580	65.9	21 503	34.1
1960	42 479	26 850	63.2	15 629	36.8
1961	33 703	22 653	67.2	11 050	32.8
1962	14 442	9 474	65.6	4 968	34.4
1963	6 987	4 419	63.2	2 568	36.8
1964	6 973	4 293	61.6	2 680	38.4
1965	6 710	4 750	70.8	1 960	29.2
1966	4 292	2 935	68.4	1 357	31.6
1967	2 653	1 855	69.9	798	30.1
1968	1 563	1 087	69.5	476	30.5
Total	646 315	353 807	65.8	185 159	34.4

[1] See A. Schmelz, „West-Ost-Migranten im geteilten Deutschland der fünfziger und sechziger Jahre", in: J. Motte, R. Ohliger and others, v. Oswald (publisher), „50 Jahre Bundesrepublik, 50 Jahre Einwanderung. Nachkriegsgeschichte als Migrationsgeschichte", special edition, Frankfurt a. M. 1999, p. 89.
[2] Settlers: west-east migrants from the FRG to the GDR with former residence in the FRG.
[3] Repatriates and settlers were first statistically recorded separately in the GDR since June 1953.

Staying Quote of West-East-Migrants who Immigrated from the FRG to the GDR since January 1, 1954 and Resided there until June 30 1961[1]

Total absolute	Total in %	Number of repatriates	Repatriates in %	Number of settlers	Settlers in %
225 565	59.3	172 939	64.9	52 626	46.1

[1] See Schmelz, „West-Ost-Migranten", l. c., p.102.

Quote of Renewed Emigrations of the West-East-Migrants from the GDR to the FRG in %[1]

Year	Total	of those repatriates	of those settlers
1959	22.2	18.8	33.6
1960	25.2	24.8	25.9
1961	44.4	45.6	41.9
1962	6.1	6.6	5.1
1963	6.0	6.7	5.0

[1] See Schmelz, „West-Ost-Migranten", l. c., p.101.

Escape/Migration Motives[1]

Motive	Before border opening (10.10.89–08.11.89)	1st phase after border opening (09.11.89–30.11.89)	2nd phase after border opening (14.12.89–31.01.90)
Lack of personal freedom	97.6	97.7	85.8
Political conditions	97.1	86.7	93.3
Low standard of living	78.2	82.4	88.0
Friends/relatives in the West	66.4	63.7	58.9
Bad working conditions	53.6	58.6	72.0

[1] See D. Voigt, H. Belitz-Demiriz and S. Meck, „Die innerdeutsche Wanderung und der Vereinigungsprozeß. Soziodemographische Struktur und Einstellungen von Flüchtlingen/Übersiedlern aus der DDR vor und nach der Grenzöffnung", in: Deutschland Archiv 23 (1990) 5, p. 742: multiple statements on the basis of 2 582 persons asked.

The Wishes of GDR-Escapees / Migrants for their New Life in the FRG[1]

Wish	Prior to the opening of the border (10.10.89–08.11.89)	1st phase after the opening of the border (09.11.89–30.11.89)	2nd phase after the opening of the border (14.12.89–31.01.90)
Personal, political and freedom of opinion	78.4	68.7	38.2
Better standard of living, supply/ housing/earnings	43.1	55.3	74.3
Freedom to travel	38.6	18.8	5.8
Better working/ living conditions	23.1	32.0	45.3

[1] See Voigt, Belitz-Demiriz, Meck, „Die innerdeutsche Wanderung", l. c., p. 744: multiple statements on the basis of 2 582 persons interviewed.

Prosecution of „Illegal Immigration"
and „Illegal Border Crossing" (§ 213 StGB-DDR)[1]

Year	Preliminary proceedings	Sentencing to imprisonment	Year	Preliminary proceedings	Sentencing to imprisonment
1958	9 997	n/a	1974	3 141	n/a
1959	3 791	n/a	1975	3 282	n/a
1960	7 798	n/a	1976	2 798	n/a
1961	9 941	n/a	1977	3 371	n/a
1962	11 780	n/a	1978	3 092	n/a
1963	8 197	n/a	1979	2 817	1 781
1964	7 814	2 373	1980	3 274	2 067
1965	7 669	3 656	1981	2 898	1 865
1966	6 903	3 598	1982	2 778	1 847
1967	n/a	3 219	1983	2 910	1 800
1968	n/a	2 978	1984	2 868	1 800
1969	n/a	2 572	1985	2 324	1 329
1970	n/a	2 424	1986	2 822	1 213
1971	4 495	2 991	1987	5 696	1 763
1972	2 887	n/a	1988	9 169	2 337
1973	3 468	n/a	1989	n/a	2 569

[1] Source: Foundation Archive of Party and Mass Organisations in the Federal Archive (BArch-SAPMO); Chief Public Prosecution Office of the GDR; here quoted from: F. Werkentin, "Recht und Justiz im SED-Staat", Bonn 1998 (= Deutsche ZeitBilder), p. 57 and p. 71.

This is the spot where the transport police-man Hans-Dieter Wesa (19) was shot after he had already reached West Berlin territory. Bösebrücke, Bornholmer Straße, Wedding, August 23, 1962

The Deaths
at the Border

Recovery of the first shot escapee Günter Litfin,
Berlin, Humboldt-Hafen, August 24, 1961

For fifty minutes, 18-year old Peter Fechter lay bleeding to death at the wall in Zimmerstraße
before the border patrols came out of their hiding places, August 17, 1962

This wooden cross honours an unknown escapee that wanted to reach West Berlin by swimming
on October 8, 1962 but was shot by border patrols. Kreuzberg/Oberbaumbrücke

Deaths at the Border[1]

Place/cause of death	Prior to 13.8.61	Since 13.8.61	Total
Berlin border/wall	37	190	227
Inner-German border	247	237	484
Baltic Sea	17	164	181
Border to Bulgaria, Czechoslovakia, Poland, Hungary (only GDR-citizens)	16	49	65
Other escape ways (skyjacking, export of goods, transit routes)	0	7	7
Members of the GDR border regime during the prevention of escapes	18	19	37
Soviet deserters	11	10	21
Shooting down air planes in the frontier zone	18	3	21
Persons liquidates after successful escape to the FRG	0	1	1
Persons fetched back after successful escape and persons executed in the GDR or the USSR or persons who died during imprisonment	12	1	13
Persons arrested during the preparation of their escape, during the escape attempt or persons who died during imprisonment	2	5	7
Ransom paid, then arrested while in transit to freedom and "deceased"	0	1	1
Total	378	687	1,065[2]

[1] See 137th press conference of the Work Group August 13 of August 12, 2004 in the house at Checkpoint Charlie, Berlin, p. 7. Names of two more fatalities made public in November 2004. Total number of cases reaches 1,067.

[2] Numerical data for comparison: portrayal of the essential tasks of the Central Investigation Office for Crimes against the State and Gang Criminality (ZERV) at the Chief of Police in Berlin of November 30, 2000, p. 4: 421 persons, that died in the frontier zone due to a prosecutable offence or omission — of those 19 youths or children.
Public Prosecutor's Office No. II at the regional court Berlin: 270 deaths altogether in the period from 1946 until 1989; see „Nachweisliche Todesfälle an der SBZ-Demarkationslinie/DDR-Staatsgrenze – einschl. Berlin – infolge Gewaltakts" of the Public Prosecutor's Office Berlin; status: June 9, 2000.

Ministry of
National Security,
1989

The Organisation of National Security in the GDR

The SSD-labour camp Hohenschön-
hausen in East Berlin, 1956

Erich Mielke, Minister of
National Security since 1957,
here at the end of the fifties

The Minstry of National Security (MfS) in East Berlin

Promotion of Erich Mielke (left) to army General by Erich Honnecker, February 1, 1980

Organisation Structure[1] of the Ministry of National Security (MfS)[2] 1989

Sevice units reporting directly to the Ministry of National Security[3]	Duty	Number of employees
Minister's Secretary	Personal care for the Minister	7
Minister's Work Group (AGM)	Mobilisation work/planning; supervision of unofficial collaborators (UC); work with officers in special deployment (OibE)	689
Guard Regime „Feliks E. Dzierzynski" (GR) (subordinate to the head of AGM)	Guard/safety regime; protection of persons and objects; honour formation; securing of demonstrations; deployment in economic measures	11 203
Central Evaluation and Information Group (ZAIG)	Recording/evaluation/analysis of information; situation assessment/statements by the Minister; evaluation of West German mass media; control of the counter-intelligence units; draft of official regulations; central planning; press/PR-work	423
Department XII (subordinate to the ZAIG)	Recording/checking of persons/objects; maintenance of the central index of persons; registration of operative processes (OP); central information MfS-internal; archiving of operative documents	344
Department XIII (independent service unit, subordinate to ZAIG)	Electronic computing centre; data processing projects; maintenance and securing of MfS with EDP-technology	449
Legal Department (independent dept., subordinate to ZAIG)	Legal/contract projects; international relations; intern. conventions; relations to the FRG/West Berlin (travel/visitor's traffic/transit agreement/traffic agreement); legal affairs	12
Management Office (BdL)	Duty organisation; documentation; classified information; postal/courier service; protocol tasks; petitions; visitor's traffic; third-party personnel management; securing of objects	324
Main Department Cadre and Training (HA KuSch)	Planning/balancing of the cadre;convincing/employment/training of new full-time collaborators; cadre advertising; caring for new military professio-nals; training/further education; development of the leadership cadre; disciplinary work; internal security	1 047
Central Medical Service (ZMD) (subordinate to HA KuSch)	Medical care for full-time collaborators; management of the hospital Berlin-Buch/outpatient clinic Berlin-Lichtenberg/prison hospital Berlin-Hohenschönhausen; management of outposts/outpatient departments; labour medicine examination office; pharmaceutical centre Berlin- Pankow	1 161
College of the MfS (subordinate to HA KuSchu)	Training of officer's candidates in college/correspondence courses to certified lawyers; vocational college/correspondence courses; qualification/further education measures; graduation to Dr. jur./Dr. sc. jur.; teaching/research; appraisal work	758

[1] Compiled from R. Wiedmann (reviser), „Die Organisationsstruktur des Ministeriums für Staatssicherheit 1989", Berlin 1995 (= MfS-handbook, vol. V/1).

[2] Created according to the law about the formation of a Ministry for National Security of 8.2.1950 (GBl. p. 95).

[3] Erich Mielke (1907–2000), 1950–1957 State Secretary in the MfS resp. from 1953–1955 Deputy State Secretary in the State Secretariat for National Security in the Ministry of the Interior; since 1957 Minister of National Security.

Main Department II (HA II)	Counter-espionage; internal security; surveillance of foreign representations; securing of the foreign representations of the GDR; instruction of the operative groups in Moscow, Warszawa, Prague, Budapest, Sofia; spying/control of the work of journalists/correspondents/privileged persons accredited in the GDR; cooperation with the SED/FDGB with German Communist Party (DKP)/Sozialist. Einheitspartei Westberlins (SEW).	1 432
Department M (subordinate to HA II)	Control/evaluation of national/international mail; establishment/investigation of secret service and subversive connections/acts of treason; prevention of the distribution of materials with an "anti-state" content; working up/compiling information about the attitude/conduct/contacts/associations of persons/ facts; maintenance of handwriting records/address file; supervision of UC; work with OibE/full-time unofficial collaborators (FUC); maintenance of own duty rooms in important post offices.	530
Main Department IX (HA IX)	Performance of the authorities of a governmental investigative organ; processing of investigation proceedings/preliminary inquiries; Investigation of „political underground activities"/„attacks against the national border "/all types of unlawful leaving of the GDR and others; processing of offences MfS/ UC/ military; Nazi/war crimes; link between the public prosecutor/courts; cooperation with the investigative organs of other Socialist countries.	484
Department X	Collaboration MfS — security organs of other Socialist countries; translation service.	46
Department XIV	Remand/execution of sentence in the MfS; securing/ control operations in the remand prisons I/II/ pri- soner's hospital of the ZMD; Ensuring checks of suspects/investigations of the departments in charge at HA IX; cooperation with justice administration organs/remand prisons of the Administration of the Penal System of the Ministry of the Interior (MdI); prisoner labour commandos; air transports/car returns from other Socialist countries; supervision of UC.	255
Finance Department	Budget administration; cash/currency management; financial control; pay/salaries/social security/payment of pensions; savings society of the MfS.	177
Office of the Central Administration of the Sports Club Dynamo	Sports organisation MdI/MfS/Customs administration.	(app.) 1400 (of those MfS) 464
Main Department Personal Safety (HA PS)	Protection of persons/care/catering for leading representatives/foreign guests; securing of surroundings; protection of objects; securing of routes/events/trips abroad; military-operative/military sport education; foreign language training; professional instruction of WR.	3 762

Duty unit subordinate to the deputy[1]	Duty	Number of collaborators
Deputy's secretariat	Secretarial tasks	6
Administration of Rearward Services (VRD)	Material-technical securing of the work of the MfS (material planning, inventory/stock keeping, construction, supplies, car services, coordination office Karlshorst); supervision UCs; work with OibE.	3 279
Main Department XVIII (HA XVIII)	Securing of central economic areas/objects/ installations; economic counter intelligence; clarification/confirmation of nomenclature cadres/ foreign/travel cadres; securing of the foreign economic relations esp. to the non-Socialist economic territory (NSW); economic crime; securing FDGB; information activities for economic processes; supervision of UC; work with OibE.	647
Main Department XIX (HA XIX)	Securing of traffic (German Reichsbahn, military traffic, civil aviation, economic aviation, cargo traffic, inland/maritime shipping, carriers, deep sea fleet, port economy); securing of mail/telephone operations; securing of border-crossing traffic; reconnaissance/confirmation of cadres; supervision of UC.	251
Main Department XX (HA XX)	Prevention/discovery/counteracting of „political-ideological diversion (PID)/„political underground activities (PUT); securing of central organs/institutions of the state; securing of leadership committees of the parties (w/o SED)/ mass organisations; youth politics; discovery/processing of "anti-state agitation"; securing of central sports installations; counter-intelligence work in competitive sports; elucidation/ processing/securing of the church and religious community; securing of central mass media (TV, radio, press, publishers); cultural politics; securing of central education installations; counter-intelligence work in the operational area (esp. FRG/West Berlin) against centres of PUT/among followers of „alternative groups"; securing of installations/facilities of the SED; supervision of UC; work with the OibE.	461
Central Work Group Protection of Classified Information (ZAGG)	Securing of the protection of secrets in the state organs/businesses/installations; control of data protection; Institute for the Protection of Confidential Information; Economy College, Berlin-Karlshorst.	58
Work Group Commercial Coordination (AG BKK)	Counter-intelligence in the area of commercial coordination (KoKo) in the Ministry of Foreign Trade; securing of subordinate foreign trade businesses/sales representatives businesses; supervision UC; work with the OibE/HIM.	120
Central Operative Staff (ZOS)	Securing of central campaigns/safeguarding operations; overview of safeguarding-policy relevant occurrences/events; operative situation centre (OLZ)	64
Work Group E (AG E)	Procurement/provision of operative/technical means/materials/equipment for the deputy section; planning/procurement/storage/maintenance of necessary materials; cooperation with the operative-technical sector (OTS)	6

[1] Rudi Mittig (1925–1994), Colonel General, since 1975 Deputy Minister of National Security.

Duty unit subordinate to the deputy [1]	Duty	Number of collaborators
Secretariat	Secretarial tasks	20
Main Department I (HA I)	Counter-espionage in the NVA and the GDR border troops; work in the operation field for the reconnaissance of the West German army, the West German border police, border customs/Bavarian border police/NATO-armies; securing of the Ministry of National Defence (MfNV)/subordinate installations; supervision of UCs; work with the OibE/ HIM.	2 319
Main Administration VI (HA VI)	Passport control; securing/control/monitoring of the entry/exit/transit traffic; data recording/central stoage/investigations of the holiday traffic; search processes/avoidance of misuses in border-crossing traffic; reconnaissance of the border crossing points FRG/West Berlin; reconnaissance of persons suspected of espionage; observation/care for political tourists; securing of objects/installations of travel/tourism; counter-espionage among the members of the GDR customs administration; supervision of UCs; work with the OibE (esp. in GDr customs admin.)	2 025
Main Administration VII (HA VII)	Securing/shielding of the MdI, esp. German People's Police (DVP), People's Police (VP), civil defence staff, task forces of the working class; cooperation with the CID; securing of the penal system administration MdI; recruiting of prisoners/people released from jail; securing of the Central Admission Home (ZAH) Röntgental; counter-espionage among home comers/resident foreigners; supervision of UCs; work with the OibE	357
Main Administration VIII (HA VIII)	Observation of persons in border-crossing holiday traffic/members of the military inspection/privileged persons/correspondents; observations PUT/political tourism; investigations/arrests/searches during operative occurrences/(central) campaigns; securing/control of transit routes; investigations/observations in the FRG/West Berlin; measures against persons/groups/installations in the "field of operation"; supervision of UCs; work with OibE.	1 618
Main Administration XXII (HA XXII)	Fight against terror; observation/examination of left and right wing terrorism in the „field of operation"; monitoring/control of internal terrorism; preventive terror defence; negotiations with hostage-takers/kidnappers; training/deployment of anti-terror forces; flight safety accompaniments; determination/securing/transport of suspicious objects (explosives).	878
Central Coordination Group (ZKG)	Control of escapes/departures/migrations to the FRG/West Berlin/non-Socialist countries; prevention/discovery of "illegal departure from the GDR" (§ 213 StGB-DDR); combating „anti-state human trafficking" (§ 105 StGB-DDR); processing/control/infiltration of UC into escape aiding organisations; cooperation with Socialist states in order to prevent spectacular escapes; generation of current overviews; supervision of UCs; deployment HIM; work with the OibE.	192
Work Group XVII	Securing of the work of the Office for Visiting and Travel Affairs of the GDR in West Berlin („Permit Offices "); supervision of UCs; work with the OibE.	308

[1] Gerhard Neiber (*1929), General Lieutenant, since 1980 Deputy Minister of National Security.

Duty unit subordinate to the deputy [1]	Duty	Number of collaborators
Secretariat	Secretarial tasks	16
Main Department III (HA III)	Radio reconnaissance/defence; control/monitoring of broadcasting nets/communication channels/ether above GDR-territory; security/observance of secrecy in GDR-communication channels; supervision of UC; work with the OibE.	2 361
Operative-Technical Sector (OTS)	Research/development work/construction of models/small series manufacturing of operative-techn. devices/installations/concealed „containers"; development of means of chem./photographic message transfer; implementation/generation of forensic/scientific expertises; examination/analysis of opponent technologies; procurement/exhibition of "operative documents"; MfS fingerprint collection.	1 131
News Department	Planning/organisation/securing of MfS-communications/communication MfS — party/state; securing of confidential government communication channels.	1 559
Department XI	Securing of the encryption system; development/production/application of new encryption technologies/procedures; decoding of foreign encryptions; supervision of UC; work with the OibE.	513
Department of Armament/Chemical Service	Securing of the MfS with arms/ammunition/chemical equipment; protection of MfS-collaborators from mass extermination weapons/nuclear accidents; radiation/poison protection; training and further training weapons technology/chem. service; arms deals.	176
Department 26 (independent)	Cooperation with the German post offices/telecommunications offices; monitoring of telecommunications/telephones/telexes; acoustic monitoring of closed/partially open spaces; optical/electronic observation/documentation esp. in rooms; application of security devices/chemical markings; recognition/reconnaissance of room surveillance devices deployed by the enemy; conspirative entry of objects; supervision UC; work with the OibE.	436

[1] Wolfgang Schwanitz (*1930), Lieutenant General, since 1986 Deputy Minister of National Security.

Department, deputy and Manager of the HV A [1]	Duty	Number of employees
Main Administration Reconnaissance (HV A)	Foreign reconnaissance/counter-espionage/ „active measures" in the field of operation (esp. FRG/ Berlin-W.)	3 819
District committee of the SED with the integrated mass organisations "Freie Dt. Jugend (FDJ)", „Freier Dt. Gewerkschaftsbund (FDGB)", „Gesell. für Dt.-Sowjet. Freundschaft (DSF)" in the MfS	Party work in the MfS	160
Total MfS Berlin incl. WR		46 341[2]

[1] Werner Großmann (*1929), Colonel General, since 1986 Deputy Minister for National Security.
[2] See the number of 47 847 full-time collaborators of the Ministry for National Security Berlin including the guard regiment Berlin for the year 1989 in the following table; reasons for the slight deviation between the two figures stated: different sources, different target dates, recording/non-recording of collaborators released for training.

Full-Time Collaborators of the[1]
Ministry for National Secutiry (MfS)[2]

Year[3]	MfS Berlin incl. GR	MfS district administration incl. district departments	MfS total
1950	n/a	n/a	2 700
1955	3 869	11 000	14 869
1960	6 151	12 320	18 471
1965	14 874	14 316	29 137[4]
1970	22 255	21 056	43 311
1975	31 557	27 957	59 514
1980	41 248	33 890	75 138
1985	46 158	38 987	85 263[5]
1989	47 847	43 168	91 015

[1]   Regular officers/regular NCOs, officers in special deployment, full-time unofficial collaborators, unknown collaborators, NCOs for a limited time/soldiers for a limited time, civil employees.
[2]   Compiled acc. to Gieseke, „Die hauptamtlichen Mitarbeiter", l. c., p. 98–101.
[3]   Status 1950–1985: December 31 each; status 1989: October 31
[4]   [recte: 29 190]
[5]   [recte: 85 145]

Unofficial Collaborators (UC)
of the Ministry for National Security[1]

Year	UC[2]	UCC[3]	SCS[4]	Total
1986	112 150	31 152	app. 32 000	app. 175 000
1987	110 846	31 588	app. 32 000	app. 174 000
1988	109 281	32 282	app. 32 000	app. 173 000[5]

[1]   See H. Müller-Enbergs, „IM-Statistik 1985–1989", Berlin 1993 (= BStU, BF informs 3/1993), p. 4–17.
[2]   Contained therein the categories UCS: UC for the political-operative penetration and securing of the area of responsibility; UCCI: UC of counter-intelligence with contacts to the enemy respectively for immediate processing in case of persons suspected to collaborate with the enemy; UCS: UC for special deployments; SUC: UC for the supervision of other UC and SCS. Not considered: UC of the MfS Headquarter Reconnaissance and the German People's Police.
[3]   UCC: UC for securing conspiracy and communication.
[4]   SCS: social collaborators for security
[5]   Suspected total of UCs in MfS counter-intelligence in October 1989.

Trial at the High Court of Justice of the GDR. On the right, chief public prosecutor Joseph Streit, in the middle the President of the High Court of Justice, Heinrich Töplitz, 1967

Injustice in the Soviet Occupied Zone (SOZ), the GDR and in East Berlin

Propaganda for compulsory collectivisation

The GDR-prison Berlin-Rummelsburg, where a high percentage of the prisoners were locked up for political reasons. Aerial photograph, 1987

This married couple only managed to demonstrate for the observance of the UN-human rights for a few minutes. Siegfried Müller was sentenced to four years, his wife Rita to two and a half years of imprisonment, their children were taken away to a children's home. 1975

With a poster campaign, these youths demanded the observance of human rights and the right of free speech in April 1974. They were expelled from the GDR.

Surveillance and blockade of Robert Havemann's house in Grünheide.

Expropriation
Property Expropriated as a Result of the Land Reform and turned over to the Land Fund[1]
(Total Area) in ha[2]

Expropriated property:	SOZ (total)	Mecklenburg	Brandenburg	Saxony-Anhalt	Saxony	Thuringia
Private property	2 649 099	861 571	739 383	572 702	302 220	173 223
State property	337 507	133 489	86 255	77 117	13 277	27 369
Settlement associations/ National Socialist institutes	22 764	4 991	10 617	4 963	1 636	557
State forests	200 247	50 139	77 309	52 026	14 121	6 632
Other property	88 465	23 388	34 265	12 949	17 554	309
Total	3 298 082	1 073 578	947 829	719 777	348 808	208 090

[1] Fund into which the properties were incorporated for redistribution.
[2] See M. Judt, „Aufstieg und Niedergang der „Trabi-Wirtschaft", in: Ders. (publisher), GDR-history in documents, decrees, reports, internal materials and everyday testimony, Berlin 1997 (= research about the GRD-society), document W 2.1., p. 103.

Expropriation
Areas in ha distributed to new Private Owners as a Result of the Land Reform
(In Brackets: Number of new Owners)[1]

Property distributed to:	SOZ (total)	Mecklenburg	Brandenburg	Saxony-Anhalt	Saxony	Thuringia
Landless farmers/ farm workers	932 487 (119 121)	365 352 (38 286)	220 276 (27 665)	218 209 (33 383)	87 289 (13 742)	41 361 (6 045)
Farmers with little land	274 848 (82 483)	41 316 (10 867)	77 582 (20 821)	71 865 (20 359)	50 865 (17 553)	33 190 (12 883)
Relocated persons[2]	763 596 (91 155)	365 943 (38 892)	208 812 (24 978)	114 227 (16 897)	51 573 (7 492)	23 041 (2 896)
Small tenant farmers	41 661 (43 231)	6 561 (3 428)	9 603 (7 004)	12 129 (12 057)	5 062 (6 516)	8 296 (14 226)
Non-agricultural workers/employees	114 665 (183 261)	19 437 (9 842)	28 409 (27 251)	33 116 (63 319)	21 142 (55 772)	12 561 (27 077)
Forest subsidies to old farmers	62 742 (39 838)	16 814 (13 204)	19 254 (8 379)	9 731 (6 374)	8 168 (5 091)	8 775 (6 590)
Total	2 189 999 (559 089)	815 423 (114 519)	563 936 (116 298)	459 287 (152 389)	224 129 (106 166)	127 224 (69 717)

[1] See Judt, „Aufstieg und Niedergang", l. c., document W 2.2.a), p. 104.
[2] This means persons expelled form the east of Germany after WW II, called „relocated persons" in the GDR.

Expropriation
Land in ha distributed to Public Corporations because of the Land Reform[1]

Property distributed to:	SOZ (total)	Mecklenburg	Brandenburg	Saxony - Anhalt	Saxony	Thuringia
State property[2]	594 580	111 929	192 553	158 135	92 920	39 043
Publicly owned goods	170 637	57 381	50 025	43 146	9 764	10 321
District property	6 037	2 144	607	1 890	671	725
Communal property[3]	198 414	47 171	64 537	40 860	18 023	27 823
Association of mutual farmer's aid[4]	39 881	21 598	3 888	9 536	2 631	2 228
Machine rental stations	913	347	181	259	71	55
Total	1 010 462	240 470	311 791	253 826	124 080	80 195

[1] See Judt, „Aufstieg und Niedergang", l. c., document W 2.2.b), p. 104.
[2] Seed cultivation and animal breeding goods, teaching and experimental facilities, fruit and tree nurseries, forests, schools and other facilities.
[3] Land for the supply of cities, open squares, town and field roads, receiving walls and bodies of water.
[4] Plots, agricultural subsidiaries, workshops and others.

Forced Collectivation
Agricultural Production Cooperatives (APC) and their Share in the Agricultural Land (AL)[1]

Year	Number of APCs	AL of the LPC in 1 000 ha	AL of the LPC in % of the Al of the GDR
1952	1 906	218	3.3
1953	n/a	754	11.6
1954	5 120	931	14.3
1955	n/a	1 279	19.7
1956	6 281	1 500	23.2
1957	n/a	1 632	25.2
1958	9 637	2 386	37.0
1959	n/a	2 897	45.1
1960	19 313	5 421	84.2
1961	n/a	5 430	84.5
1962	16 624	n/a	85.6
1964	15 861	n/a	85.7
1966	14 216	n/a	86.0
1968	11 513	n/a	85.7
1970	9 009	n/a	85.7

[1] Source: Statistic Yearbook of the GDR, here compiled and quoted from F. Werkentin, "Politische Strafjustiz in der Ära Ulbricht. Vom bekennenden Terror zur verdeckten Repression", 2nd revised edition, Berlin 1997 (= research about the GDR-society), p. 375 and C. Kleßmann, „Zwei Staaten, eine Nation. Deutsche Geschichte 1955–1970", 2nd revised and augmented edition, Bonn 1997 (= series of publications by the Federal Office of Political Education, vol. 343), p. 318.

Nationalisation
Types of Ownership, Industrial Companies[1]
Number of Companies

Year	Total	Socialist	Semi-national	Private
1956	18 344	5 922	144	12 278
1959	16 791	5 131	3 534	7 826
1963	14 861	4 658	5 384	4 819
1967	13 159	3 705	5 562	3 892
1969	12 255	3 193	5 646	3 416
1971	11 253	2 619	5 658	2 976
1973	10 200			
1975	8 477			
1976	7 254			
1977	6 480			
1979	5 707			
1982	4 029			

[1] Source: Statistical Yearbook of the GDR, here quoted from: „DDR-Handbuch", vol. 2, l. c., p. 1499. Please note: since the transformation of almost all semi-national and private industrial and construction companies as well as the industrially producing crafts enterprises to national property in 1972, the companies were no longer listed according to types of ownership. Included are combine companies, as they represent independent planning and clearing units.

Nationalisation
Workers and Employees at Industrial Companies
(In 1 000 Persons)[1]

Year	Total	Socialist	Semi-national	Private
1956	2 539.7	2 113.1	14.3	412.2
1959	2 762.4	2 301.6	240.5	220.3
1963	2 775.0	2 316.0	340.5	118.6
1967	2 746.5	2 305.0	349.2	92.2
1969	2 818.8	2 379.3	359.9	79.5
1971	2 825.4	2 410.1	348.1	67.2
1973	3 004.0	n/a	n/a	n/a
1974	3 022.1	n/a	n/a	n/a
1975	3 032.8	n/a	n/a	n/a
1976	3 071.1	3 068.8	0.1	2.3
1977	3 082.9	3 080.7	0.0	2.2
1979	3 120.6	3 118.0	0.0	1.7
1982	3 190.3	3 172.3	0.0	1.6

[1] Source: Statistical Yearbook of the GDR; here quoted from: "DDR-Handbuch", vol. 2, l. c., p. 1499.

Nationalisation
Output Private Trade/
Production Trade Cooperative (PTC)[1]

Year	Total output in million M	of that PTC in million M	in %	Private trade in million M	in %
1950	4.42	—	—	4.42	100.0
1953	6.04	0.01	0.2	6.03	99.8
1955	7.84	0.03	0.3	7.81	99.7
1960	9.93	2.92	29.4	7.01	70.6
1965	12.60	5.05	40.4	7.51	59.8
1970	17.76	8.86	49.9	8.90	50.1

[1] Source: Statistical year book of the GDR; here quoted from: Kleßmann, "Zwei Staaten, eine Nation", l. c., p. 315.

Nationalisation
Retail Trade Turnovers acc. to Types of Ownership
(Including Turnovers of the Catering Trade)[1]

Year	Total	Socialist trade	Of those trade organisations	Of those co-ops	Private trade (incl. factorage)
			in billions of M		
1950	17.3	8.2	5.2	3.0	9.1
1955	31.7	21.6	12.8	8.8	10.1
1960	45.0	34.8	19.8	15.0	10.2
1971	67.1	54.6	30.6	24.0	12.5
1977	90.5	79.4	47.2	32.2	11.1
1980	100.0	88.3	53.6	34.8	11.7
1982	103.5	91.5	55.5	35.9	12.0
			shares in %		
1950	100.0	47.4	30.1	17.3	52.6
1955	100.0	68.1	40.4	27.8	31.9
1960	100.0	77.3	43.9	33.3	22.7
1971	100.0	81.4	45.6	35.8	18.6
1977	100.0	87.7	52.1	35.6	12.3
1980	100.0	88.3	53.6	34.8	11.7
1982	100.0	88.4	53.6	34.7	11.6

[1] Source: Statistical Yearbook of the GDR; here quoted from: "DDR-Handbuch", vol. 1, l. c., p. 237. The share of the socialist trade in the retail trade turnover only grew miniscule from the middle/end of the eighties until the downfall of the GDR, while the share of the private trade only declined to the same extent — see Judt, "Aufstieg und Niedergang", l. c., document W 27, p. 123.

Forced Resettlements along the Inner-German Border[1]
Relocated Persons from the Restricted Area
„Operation Vermin ", May 1952

District	District inhabitants	Planned resettlements families	Planned resettlements persons	Executed resettlements families	Executed resettlements persons
Oelsnitz	7 472	101	335	100	332
Plauen	2 055	67	224	66	214
Schleiz	17 950	127	450	103	382
Saalfeld	12 581	58	200	54	186
Sonneberg	31 485	280	850	115	381
Hildburghausen	33 429	70	246	81	283
Meiningen	6 186	119	497	118	494
Bad Salzungen	26 412	267	991	117	384
Eisenach	35 282	239	696	73	284
Mühlhausen	5 955	111	375	91	343
Worbis	28 149	132	508	91	336
Nordhausen	23 173	167	534	124	467
Wernigerode	23 761	86	299	85	297
Osterburg	2 178	61	194	60	229
Gardelegen	14 512	168	494	156	470
Haldensleben	26 213	131	463	125	442
Salzwedel	13 332	113	412	114	416
Oschersleben	14 611	109	281	94	294
Westprignitz	6 372	45	155	43	148
Ludwigslust	6 395	71	225	70	222
Grevesmühlen	18 419	161	621	150	529
Hagenow	31 357	242	940	222	813
Schwerin	1 988	95	385	95	385
Demarcation line	389 267	3 020	10 375	2 347	8 331

[1]   Source: BArch-SAPMO, Central Party Archive, here quoted from: I. Bennewitz and R. Potratz, „Zwangsaussied-lungen an der innerdeutschen Grenze. Analysen und Dokumente", Berlin 1994 (= research regarding GRD-history, vol. 4), p. 246.

Compulsory Resettlements at the Inner-German Border[1]
Vacant Agricultural Enterprises and Areas
„Operation Vermin", May 1952

District	Farmers in the district	Agricultural areas in the district in ha	Vacant enterprises	Vacant agricultural areas in ha
Oelsnitz	784	6 309,38	43	392.10
Plauen	286	3 342,50	34	546.59
Schleiz	1 033	7 006,11	34	269.10
Saalfeld	2 510	3 643,00	16	148.11
Sonneberg	1 689	8 256,00	79	691.00
Hildburghausen	3 392	21 003,62	75	568.43
Meiningen	53	414,68	53	414.68
Bad Salzungen	2 263	15 718,00	107	868.51
Eisenach	4 883	13 724,37	100	327.62
Mühlhausen	379	2 429,00	23	108.53
Worbis	2 912	19 839,00	96	828.68
Nordhausen	2 305	11 650,25	24	301.72
Wernigerode	1 239	12 303,47	10	230.28
Osterburg	229	3 853,37	54	933.80
Gardelegen	1 059	12 804,41	61	1 306.87
Haldensleben	933	14 086,00	19	599.26
Salzwedel	2 153	20 922,53	78	1 433.56
Oschersleben	779	9 350,69	16	630.56
Westprignitz	523	7 274,66	16	335.46
Ludwigslust	415	2 891,79	11	109.15
Grevesmühlen	1 414	13 969,01	68	1 304.64
Hagenow	2 870	29 778,00	128	2 556.60
Schwerin	294	2 887,61	55	581.28
Demarcation line	34 397	243 457,45	1 200	15 486.53

[1]   Source: Federal Archive SAPMO; Central party archive; here quoted from: Bennewitz, Potratz, „Zwangs-aussiedlungen", l. c., p. 247.

Compulsory Resettlements at the Inner-German Border[1]
Resettled Inhabitants of the Restricted Areas
„Consolidation Campaign", October 1961

District	Inhabitants	Resettled persons	Resettled relatives	Total resettlements	Resettled persons in % of the inhabitants of the districts
Grevesmühlen	10 959	57	145	202	1.84
Gadebusch	3 073	16	49	65	2.12
Hagenow	28 805	107	242	349	1.21
Ludwigslust	10 298	78	226	304	2.95
Seehausen	2 086	3	11	14	0.67
Salzwedel	7 401	15	48	63	0.85
Klötze	14 558	13	28	41	0.28
Haldensleben	14 131	21	51	72	0.51
Oschersleben	17 191	25	51	76	0.44
Halberstadt	14 109	19	33	52	0.37
Wernigerode	17 125	16	38	54	0.32
Nordhausen	8 626	30	78	108	1.25
Worbis	8 370	16	48	64	0.76
Heiligenstadt	10 865	43	104	147	1.35
Eisenach	23 065	42	90	132	0.57
Mühlhausen	5 396	34	91	125	2.32
Suhl	97 451	164	398	562	0.58
Bad Salzungen	13 358	29	87	116	0.87
Meiningen	15 446	39	105	144	0.93
Hildburghausen	16 330	33	78	111	0.68
Sonneberg	47 947	54	114	168	0.35
Neuhaus	4 370	9	14	23	0.53
Lobenstein	9 896	73	181	254	2.57
Schleiz	7 948	58	156	214	2.69
Saalfeld	4 388	32	67	99	2.26
Plauen	1 680	19	45	64	3.81
Oelsnitz	3 719	39	75	114	3.07
Demarcation Line	321 140	920	2 250	3 175	0.99

[1] Source: The Federal Commissioner for the documents of the Ministry of National Security of the former German Democratic Republic (BStU); here quoted from: Bennewitz, Potratz, "Zwangsaussiedlungen", l. c., p. 285. Numerous apartments and houses were evacuated in several large-scale operations between September 1961 and August 1962 in Berlin (East) and the GDR along the urban Berlin sector boundary. A total of 3 835 persons were afflicted by these measures — see "Ulbrichts Mauer", l. c., p. 14.

Soviet Camps in the SOZ/GDR 1945–1950[1]

Camp	Internal Soviet name	Utilisation prior to May 1945	Period of existence	Total occupation	Average occupation	Deaths	Deportations to the USSR	Releases 1948 and before	Releases 1950	Prisoner categories
Bautzen	Special camp no. 4 as of 1948 no. 3	Prison	May 1945–Febr. 1950	23 000–30 000	5 000–9 000	4 100–16 700	4 000–8 650	app. 5 000	742	Interned prisoners
Berlin-Hohen-schönhausen	Special camp no. 3	Large kitchen, factory grounds	May 1945–Oct. 1946	10 000–12 500	app. 2 000	3 000–3 500	—	—	—	Interned prisoners
Buchenwald	Special camp no. 2	Concentration camp	Aug. 1945–Febr. 1950	28 445	10 000–12 000	6 000–8 000	1 330–2 100	9 250	7 153	Internees
Frankfurt/Oder	?	Settlement „A. d. Wachsbleibe" „Horn"-barracks	May–Oct. 1945 / May 1945–Sept./Oct. 1947	app. 10 500	6 000–8 000	app. 8 000	?	—	—	Interned POWs
Fünfeichen near Neubran-denburg	Special camp no. 9	POW-camp	Apr. 1945–Oct. 1948	17 200–20 000	app. 8 000	3 000–8 700	500–1 000	4 000–4 500	—	Internees
Jamlitz near Lieberose	Special camp no. 6	Penal camp of the SS	Sept. 1945–Apr. 1947	10 000–14 200	5 000–6 000	4 000–5 200	app. 1 000	—	—	Interned POWs
Ketschendorf near Fürsten-walde	Special camp no. 5	Worker settlement	Apr. 1945–Febr. 1947	15 000–20 000	app. 6 200	5 300–7 600	app. 2 000	—	—	Interned POWs
Mühlberg near Riesa	Special camp no. 1	POW-camp	Sept. 1945–Oct. 1948	21 835	app. 12 000	7 000–8 800	app. 3 075	4 500–7 300	—	Internees
Sachsenhausen	Special camp no. 7 as of 1948 no. 1	Concentration camp	Aug. 1945–March 1950	50 000–60 000	11 000–12 000	app. 12 000	7 000–10 300	3 400–6 000	6 617	Interned prisoners, POWs until 1946
Fort Zinna/Torgau	Special camp no. 10 / Special camp no. 8	Military prison / „Seydlitz"-barracks	May/June 1946–Oct. 1948 / Aug. 1945–March 1947	28 814 / app. 8 600	app. 3 000 / appr. 6 000	app. 2 000[2]	24 050 / ?	441	—	Soviet citizens, interned prisoners POWs
Weesow near Werneuchen	Special camp no. 7	Farmstead	Mai–Aug. 1945	9 000–13 700	app. 6 000	1 000–1 500	app. 1 000	—	—	Internees

[1] See „Im Namen des Volkes?", l. c., p. 42.
[2] Total figures for both detention camps acc. to K. W. Fricke, „Politik und Justiz in der DDR. Zur Geschichte der politischen Verfolgung 1945–1968". Report and documentation. Cologne 1979, p. 79.

The Proceedings of Waldheim acc. to the Internal Final Report of 5.7.1950[1]

Total	Postpone-ments	up to 5 years	5–10 years	10–15 years	15–25 years	Life sentence	Death
3 392	84	14	371	916	1 829	146	32
in %							
100	2.5	0.4	10.9	27	54	4.3	0.9

[1] Source: BArch-SAPMO; here quoted from: Werkentin, „Recht und Justiz", l. c., p. 13.

GDR-Prisoners[1]

1953*	36 186	1970	21 717
1954	39 440	1971	25 732
1955	39 920	1972*	11 464
1956*	20 743	1973	25 977
1957	22 760	1974	30 905
1958	31 850	1975	29 488
1959	28 739	1976	25 297
1960*	18 198	1977	28 760
1961	30 124	1978	31 345
1962	19 671	1979*	20 468
1963	22 806	1980	35 591
1964*	14 221	1981	35 968
1965	18 058	1982	35 296
1966	21 105	1983	34 067
1967	24 578	1984	32 667
1968	20 552	1985	28 623
1969	20 731	1986	28 038

* Premature releases (amnesties, pardons), concerning 10 000 persons and more.

[1] Source: BArch Bln., dept. DDR; here quoted from: „Im Namen des Volkes?", l. c., p. 212; Status: each at the end of the year.

Number of Political Prisoners acc. to Categories[1]

Prisoner category	Number	Deceased, partially executed
Special camp prisoners (not sentenced)	at least 127 000 (estimates up to 200 000)	at least 43 000 (estimates up to 80 000)
People deported to the USSR from the SOC/GDR and Eastern Europe	at least 230 000	about one third
Sentenced civilians Soviet military tribunals (SMT)	more than 50 000	unknown so far
Soldiers sentenced by the SMT	more than 30 000	unknown so far
People convicted by GDR-courts	about 200 000	probably several thousand

[1] See K.-D. Müller, „Jeder kriminelle Mörder ist mir lieber ..."Imprisonment conditions for political prisoners in the SOZ and the GDR and their changes from 1945–1989, in: Ders. and A. Stephan (publishers), "Die Vergangenheit läßt uns nicht los." Imprisonment conditions for political prisoners in the SOZ and the GDR and their effects on the state of health, Berlin 1998, p. 24.

Number of Political Prisoners acc. to Time Periods[1]

Time period	Number of political prisoners per year	Estimated share of political prisoners in the total of prisoners
1950–1955	app. 11 000–14 000	app. 1/3
1956–1964	app. 6 000–7 000	app. 1/5 bis knapp 1/4
1965–1969	7 570	app. 1/3
1970–1974	5 826	app. 1/4
1975–1979	4 200	app. 1/5 bis 1/4
1980–1984	4 448	app. 1/5
1985–1988	3 862	app. 1/6

[1] See Müller, „Jeder kriminelle Mörder ...", l. c., p. 25.

Subjective Burdening as a Result of the Imprisonment Conditions of Political Prisoners (1975–1989)[1]

(n=55) in %

Helplessness against discrimination	35
Solitary confinement	25
Uncertainty	22
Intrigues among fellow prisoners	20
No contact to the outside world	20
Imprisoned although innocent	20
Cell monitoring and spying	26
General harassment	18
Everything	18
Confined rooms	16
Imprisoned together with criminals	13
Bad nutrition and hygienic conditions	11

[1] See Müller, „Jeder kriminelle Mörder ...", l. c., p. 211.

Death Sentenced by German Authorities in the SOZ/GDR[1]

Time period	Sentences	Proven executions
1945–1982[2]	372	206

[1] See E. Neubert, „Politische Verbrechen in der DDR", in: S. Courtois and others (publishers), „Das Schwarzbuch des Kommunismus. Unterdrückung, Verbrechen und Terror", 2nd edition, Munich and Zurich 1998, p. 865 pp, referring to details by F. Werkentins — see there, p. 959.
[2] Last proven execution: 1981; abolishment of the death penalty in the GDR: 1987.

Up to 1 million people demonstrated in East Berlin for freedom of press and opinion as well as democratic reforms, November 4, 1989

On June 17, 1953, East Berlin workers marched to the government building in Leipziger Straße to demonstrate for free elections and better living conditions

Enraged demonstrators tried to stop Soviet tanks in Leipziger Straße by throwing stones on June 17, 1953

Human chain between the American and the Soviet embassy in East Berlin, September 1, 1983

A vigil in Gethsemane-Church for imprisoned demonstrators, October 4, 1989

Up to 500,000 people participated in the "Monday Demonstrations" in Leipzig in the fall of 1989

Posters and banners in front of the main entrance of the People's Chamber of the GDR in East Berlin, November 5, 1989

Final rally of the largest demonstration in the history of the GDR on November 4, 1989 on Alexanderplatz in Berlin

The People's Uprising of June 17, 1953

Places	Demonstrations	Civil uprisings	Attempted or successful prisoner liberations	Deployment of Soviet military[1]
District capitals	7	6	4	13
Regional capitals	43	22	12	51
Other cities and towns	105	44	8	57
Places total	155	72	24	121

[1] Source: Federal Ministry for All-German Questions; here quoted from: 17 June 1953, published by the All-German Institute, 2nd augmented edition, Bonn, no year (= seminar material regarding the German question), p. 8.

East Berlin city district	Number of employees	Walkouts[1]
Mitte	4 413	3 300
Prenzlauer Berg	3 041	410
Friedrichshain	10 815	10 484
Treptow	8 381	5 246
Köpenick	24 037	12 598
Lichtenberg	3 640	1 288
Pankow	5 920	2 000
Weißensee	3 175	1 330
Total	63 422	36 656

[1] Source: State Archive Berlin (LArchBln); FDGB District Board Berlin; here quoted from: W. Ribbe, "Der 17. Juni 1953 in Berlin. Vorgeschichte, Verlauf und politische Folgen", in: Berlin 17. Juni 1953. Catalogue of an exhibition by the State Archive Berlin, June 17 until December 15, 1993, Berlin 1993, p. 58.

Locations	Number of companies	Number of employees[1]
Strikes/walkouts in and around East Berlin		
Soviet sector	24	27 000
Hennigsdorf	5	14 000
Ludwigsfelde	2	6 000
Potsdam	3	5 000
Teltow	3	9 000
Total	37	61 000
In the Central German industrial area		
Bitterfeld	7	58 000
Halle	9	10 000
Leipzig	6	8 000
Merseburg (Leuna/Buna)	2	45 000
Total	24	121 000
Magdeburg	16	38 000
Jena	4	18 000
Gera	11	6 000
Brandenburg/ Havel	12	13 000
Görlitz	6	10 000
Total	110	267 000

[1] Source: Federal Ministry for All-German Questions; here quoted from: "17. Juni 1953". Published by the All-German Institute, l. c., p. 8.

Arrested demonstrators in East Berlin and the GDR	Number	in %[1]
Workers	3 456	65,2
Employees	688	13,0
Self-employed craftsmen	228	4,2
Collective farm workers	17	0,3
Small and medium-sized farmers	104	1,9
Large farmers	24	0,4
Entrepreneurs	21	0,4
Unemployed	89	1,7
Others	669	12,6
Total	5 296	100,0

[1] Source: State Archive Berlin; Ministry of the Interior of the GDR; here quoted from: T. Diedrich, "Der 17. Juni 1953 in der DDR. Bewaffnete Gewalt gegen das Volk", Berlin 1991, p. 300.

Sentences passed by the GDR-Courts until October 5, 1953 in Connection with the Events on June 17, 1953[1]

Sentence	Persons
Imprisonment up to 1 year	468
Imprisonment 1–5 years	619
Imprisonment 5–10 years	87
Imprisonment over 10 years	14
Life sentences	4
Death sentences	2
Other sentences	46
Total	1 240

[1] Source: Archive for Foreign Politics of the Russian Federation. Report of the High Commissioner of the USSR about the political and economic situation of the GDR in the 3rd quarter 1953; here quoted from: Werkentin, "Politische Strafjustiz", l. c., p. 149.

Deaths in Connection with the Events on June 17, 1953[1]

Place	Persons
Berlin	39
District of Magdeburg	28
District of Leipzig	11
District of Gera	2
District of Potsdam	2
District of Halle	12
District of Frankfurt/Oder	1
District of Dresden	1
District of Schwerin	1
District of Cottbus	1
Unable to assign	11
Total	109

[1] See the paper about the event of the Work Group 13th August of June 14, 1993 at the House at Checkpoint Charlie, Berlin, p. 2.

Persons who died in Connection with the Events on June 17, 1953[1]

Death	Persons
On-the-spot executed Soviet soldiers	41
On-the-spot executed GDR-citizens	18
Executed GDR-citizens	2
Demonstrators that died of bullet wounds	27
Non-involved spectators that died of bullet wounds	3
Members of the People's Army/The MfS killed by demonstrators	4
Other deaths	14
Total	109

[1] See the paper about the event of the Work Group 13th August of June 14, 1993 at the House at Checkpoint Charlie, Berlin, p. 2.

Demonstrations

Demonstrations	Place	Time	Participators	Consequences
„White Circle"[1]	Jena	Summer 1983	initially 30, in the end 184	Approval of exit permits.
Human chain between the American and the Soviet embassy[2]	Berlin (East)	September 1, 1983	app. 50	Break-up of the demonstration through the police.
PM-12 replacement ID-card[3]	Jena	Spring 1984	app. 30–40	More careful issuance of PM-12 replacement ID-cards.
Monday demonstrations[4]	Leipzig	Fall 1989	initially 8 000, in the end 500 000	Contribution to the downfall of the GDR.
Monday demonstrations[5]	Leipzig	Fall 1989	Spec. groups of demonstrators	Protection of the MfS-headquarter from enraged demonstrators.
Large demonstration	Berlin (East)	November 4, 1989	500 000[6]– 1 000 000[7]	Contribution to the downfall of the GDR.
Storming of the MfS-headquarter[8]	Berlin (East), Normannen-straße	January 15, 1990	Tens of thousands	Partial havoc.

[1] Demonstrators dressed in white that arranged themselves in a circle on Saturdays from nine until ten AM on the „Platz der Kosmonauten" – see R. Hildebrandt, "Von Gandhi bis Walesa. Gewaltfreier Kampf für Menschenrechte", 23.–30. thousand, Berlin 1993, p. 152 pp.

[2] See Hildebrandt, „Von Gandhi bis Walesa", l. c., p. 164.

[3] At the beginning/in the middle of the eighties, around 60 000 GDR-citizens who were willing to leave their country had their regular ID-cards confiscated. They received the so-called PM-12 replacement ID that was tied to numerous conditions, above all the prohibition to leave their place of residence. The demonstrators hung their PM-12 replacement ID around their necks and showed it off — see "DER TAGESSPIEGEL" of May 19, 1984 and Hildebrandt, "Von Gandhi bis Walesa", l. c., p. 155.

[4] See B. Lindner, „Die demokratische Revolution in der DDR 1989/90", Bonn 1998 (= German ZeitBilder).

[5] See Hildebrandt, „Von Gandhi bis Walesa", l. c., p. 178.

[6] See E. Neubert, „Geschichte der Opposition in der DDR 1949–1989", 2nd revised, augmented and corrected edition, Bonn 2000 (= series of publications by the Federal Office of Political Education, vol. 346), p. 874 that speaks of over half a million people.

[7] See „Der Große Ploetz", l. c., p. 1431.

[8] See H. G. Lehmann, „Deutschland-Chronik 1945 bis 2002", Bonn 2000 (= series of publications by the Federal Office of Political Education, vol. 366), p. 386.

Resistance Groups

Group	Place	Time	Participants	Measure	Consequences
Werdau High School Students [1] „	Werdau/ Saxony	1950/1951	19	Leaflet campaigns	Sentenced to partially many years of imprisonment
Eisenberg Circle [2]	Eisenberg/ Thuringia	1953–1958	appr. 30	Graffiti leaflet campaigns, acts of sabotage	Sentenced to partially many years of imprisonment

[1] See A. Beyer, Werdauer Oberschüler, in: H.-J. Veen and others (publisher), „Lexikon Opposition und Widerstand in der SED-Diktatur", Berlin and Munich 2000, p. 373f.

[2] See P. v. z. Mühlen, „Der „Eisenberger Kreis". Jugendwiderstand und Verfolgung in der DDR 1953–1958", Bonn 1995 (= Research institute of Friedrich-Ebert-Stiftung, series: political and social history, vol. 41).

Church

Person [1]	Place	Time	Measures	Consequences
Ev. pastor Oskar Brüsewitz [2] (1929–1976)	Zeitz	18 August 1976	Self-burning	Death
Ev. pastor Joachim Gauck (* 1940)	Mecklenburg	Eighties	Participation in peace, human rights and environmental groups	Manipulation by the MfS (Ministry of National Security, Stasi).
Religion sociologist Ehrhart Neubert (* 1940)	Thuringia Berlin	Seventies/ eighties	Participation in clerical peace groups	Conflicts with governmental and clerical authorities.
Ev. pastor Rainer Eppelmann (* 1943)	Berlin (East)	Eighties	Blues masses, participation in clerical peace and human rights groups	Manipulation by the MfS (Ministry of National Security, Stasi).
Ev. pastor Dietmar Linke (*1944)	Berlin (East)	1982/1983	Co-founder of different clerical peace groups; participation/arrest in/during the human chain from the Soviet to the US-embassy, September 1, 1983	Expatriation and forced to depart to Berlin (West) 1983.

[1] See the biographical details at H. Müller-Enbergs, J. Wielgohs and D. Hoffmann (publishers.), "Wer war wer in der DDR?" Ein bibliographisches Lexikon, Berlin 2000.

[2] For similar reasons like those of Brüsewitz, the pastors Karl Erich Müller (Hadmersleben near Magdeburg, 1976) and Rolf Burgemeister (Rathenow, 1984) also voluntarily took their own lives.

Intellectuals/Artists

Person[1]	Place	Time	Measures	Consequences
Physicist-chemist Robert Havemann (1910–1982)	Berlin (East)	Sixties, seventies, eighties	System-critical readings and publications	Barred from his profession, surveillance, house arrest.
Social ecologist Rudolf Bahro (1935–1997)	Berlin (East)	Seventies	System-critical publications	Detention, discharged to the Federal Republic of Germany.
Songwriter Wolf Biermann (* 1936)	Berlin (East)	Sixties, seventies	System-critical songs and publications	Prohibited to appear in public, expatriation.
Writer Jürgen Fuchs (1950–1999)	Berlin (East)	Seventies	Different protest campaigns, system-critical publications	Expelled from the SED, degree dissertation turned down, taken off the register at Humboldt-University Berlin, detained by the MfS, expatriation.
Film director Freya Klier (* 1950)	Berlin (East)	Sixties to eighties	Attempted illegal border crossing, system-critical theatre productions, participation in peace groups	Imprisonment, barred from performing her profession, involuntary expatriation together with St. Krawczyk.
Writer Lutz Rathenow (* 1952)	Jena Berlin (East)	Seventies, eighties	Different protest campaigns, system-critical publications, participation in peace and civil rights groups	Taken off the register at Jena University, publication restrictions, arrest.
Journalist Roland Jahn (* 1953)	Jena	Seventies, eighties	Different protest campaigns, support of the Polish union Solidarnosc, participation in peace groups	Taken off the register at Jena University, manipulated by the MfS, imprisonment, expatriation and forced deportation.
Songwriter and writer Stephan Krawczyk (* 1955)	Berlin (East)	Eighties	Different protest campaigns, system-critical songs and publications	Barred from performing his profession, imprisonment, forced departure together with F. Klier.
Artist community Mecklenburg, code name „Mask"[2]	Mecklenburg	1980/1981	Plans for the founding of an artist community with 5 persons	Prevention of the project through government organs.

[1]   See the biographical details in Müller-Enbergs, Wielgohs and Hoffmann, „Wer war wer in der DDR? Ein biographisches Lexikon", Berlin 2000 l. c.
[2]   See M. Morgner, "Deckname „Maske". Die Künstlergemeinschaft Mecklenburg 1980/81". A documentation, Berlin 1995 (= series of publications by the Robert-Havemann-Archive, vol. 2).

Civil Rights/Peace/Environmental Groups

Group/ initiative[1]	Founding	(Founding) members/ institution	Place/ area	Motto/campaign/goal
Riesa Civil Rights Initiative (group/initiative)	1976	K. H. Nitschke and an additional 32 Riesa inhabitants	Riesa/ Saxony	Petition for the full obtainment of human rights with the goal of leaving the GDR for religious, political, familiar or humanitarian reasons.
Peace Decades (annual ten-day programme)	1980	Evangelical church	GDR-wide	Generating peace without weapons, turning swords into ploughshares.
Social Peace Service (initiative)	1980	Building soldiers, Evangelical church	Originally in Dresden, then all across the GDR	Creation of a civil service as an alternative to armoured or non-armoured military service.
Women for Peace (group)	1982	B. Bohley, K. Havemann, A. Ilsen, I. Kukutz, U. Poppe, B. Rathenow, K. Teichert, B. Linke, R. Mehner, H. Offner, E. Westendorf, A. Böttger, B. Harembski, R. Kibelka, G. Metz, A. Quasdorf, J. Seidel and many others	Berlin (East)	Protest against the GDR military service law of 1982, against the militarization of society, engagement for disarmament and détente, awareness of topics relevant to women, the environment and other social areas.
Jena Peace Community (group)	1982	M. Domaschk, R. Jahn and many others	Jena	Engagement for peace.
Concretely for Peace (annual several day seminar)	1983	Evangelical church	Berlin (East) Eisenach Schwerin Stendal Leipzig-Connewitz Cottbus Greifswald	Raising the awareness for problems regarding peace themes, the conditions in the GDR, the human rights question, environmental questions, the right to resistance. Demands for disarmament, détente, democratisation, rule of law, freedom.
Initiative for Peace and Human Rights (group)/ "Grenzfall" (monthly publication)	1986	M. Birthler, B. Bohley, F. Eigenfeld, W. Fischer, K. Havemann, R. Hirsch, K. & St. Hilsberg, U. &. G. Poppe, R. &. W. Templin and many others.	Berlin (East)	Open declaration of belief in a political opposition, the idea of a civil society, generation of an SED-critical counter-public, engagement for freedom, human rights and democracy.

Work Group Solidary Church (twice-annual general meeting and 10-person internal speaker's council between the general meetings)	1986	Evangelical church	Originally in Wittenberg, later all over the GDR	Striving for a church union, emancipation and democracy, enforcement of human rights near and far, ecologising society, the quest for a new lifestyle.
Environment Library Berlin (library, gallery, editor's office, print shop)/ „Umweltblätter" (magazine)	1986	H. Simon, T. Sello, W. Rüddenklau, B. Schlegel and many more.	Berlin (East)	Raising awareness for the problems of peace and environment subjects, information networking and publishing all essential oppositional activities of the Berlin action groups.
Church from the Bottom (initiative)	1987	R. Schult, V. Lengsfeld, H. Mißlitz, S. Ahrens, K. Harich, U. Kulisch, Th. Grund and many more.	Originally in Berlin (East) later all over the GDR	Church reform, participation in other oppositional groups.
Green Ecological Network Arch in the Evangelic Church (federally structured regional groups)/ Arche Nova (magazine)	1988	C. Jordan, Ch. Schult, M. Voigt, F. Zimmermann and many more.	GDR-wide	Raising awareness for the problems of environmental destruction, the death of forests, the decay of the cities, the waste of energy and mass animal farming.

[1] See Veen, "Lexikon Opposition und Widerstand", l. c.

The Berlin Wall
at Brandenburg
gate on the day
after its opening,
November 10,
1989

The Brandenburg Gate on November 10, 1989

and on November 11, 1989

Die Mauer. Zahlen. Daten

Oberbaumbrücke on November 10, 1989

Chronological Table[*]

1945

May 8	The Second World War, instigated by Hitler, ends with the unconditional surrender of Germany.
June 5	Takeover of the highest governmental power in Germany by the USSR, USA, Great Britain and France. Division of Germany into four occupied zones and division of Berlin into four sectors.
June 9	Order no. 1 about the formation of the Soviet Military Administration in Germany (SMAD).
June 10	Order no. 2 of the SMAD about the admission of anti-fascist democratic parties and labour unions in the Soviet zone.
July 1	Establishment of the "German People's Police" under control of the SMAD.
July 1-3	Withdrawal of the American and British troops from Saxony, Thuringia and Mecklenburg, entry in Berlin's west sectors.
July 9	Order no. 5 of the SMAD about the creation of five states respectively provinces in the Soviet zone.
July 17-August 2	Potsdam conference of the major powers about the handling of conquered Germany.
July 23	Order no. 10 of the SMAD about the seizure of all banks, savings banks and insurance companies.
July 27	Order no. 17 of the SMAD about the establishment of eleven German central administrations.
September 3-11	Regulations of the state and province administrations about the implementation of the land reform in the Soviet zone, by which large estates above 100 ha are expropriated without compensation.
October 22	The state and province administrations receive the right from the SMAD to pass laws and decrees with legal force.
December 19	The SMAD dismisses leading CDU members because of their rejection of the expropriation without compensation in the land reform and confirms their successors.

1946

March 31	In a ballot of the West Berlin SPD, 82% decline a merger with the KPD.
April 19-20	The 15th party conference of the KPD and the 40th party conference of the SPD

[*] See

Berlin. 13. August. Sperrmaßnahmen gegen Recht und Menschlichkeit, hrsg. v. Bundesministerium für gesamt-deutsche Fragen, 2., durchges. u. erg. Aufl., Bonn und Berlin 1963, p. 4–14.

DDR-Handbuch, Bd. 2, hrsg. v. Bundesministerium für innerdeutsche Beziehungen, 3., überarb. u. erw. Aufl., Köln: Verlag Wissenschaft und Politik 1985, p. 1560–1615.

Enzyklopädie der DDR. Personen, Institutionen und Strukturen in Politik, Wirtschaft, Justiz, Wissenschaft und Kultur. Berlin: Directmedia 2000 (= Digitale Bibliothek, Bd. 32), „Chronik der SBZ/DDR".

Fischer, Wolfgang Georg und Fritz von der Schulenburg, Die Mauer. Monument des Jahrhunderts, mit einer Chronologie von Hans-Jürgen Dyck, Berlin: Ernst & Sohn 1990, Anhang.

Schroeder, Klaus, Der SED-Staat. Partei, Staat und Gesellschaft 1949–1990, München: Propyläen 2000, Chroniken zu Beginn eines jeden Kapitels.

Weber, Hermann (Hrsg.), DDR. Dokumente zur Geschichte der Deutschen Demokratischen Republik 1945–1985, München: dtv 1986 (= dtv dokumente, Bd. 2953), p. 407–445. 1946

	agree upon compulsory unification to form the Socialist Unity Party of Germany (SED).
Sep 30 - Oct 1	Sentencing of the main war criminals in Nuremberg.
October 20	Elections to the five state parliaments and the district parliaments in the Soviet Zone. The SED receives 47.5% of the votes. In the elections for the Berlin city parliament, the SED only receives 19.8% of the votes.

1947

March 10 - April 24	Conference of the foreign ministers of the USA, Great Britain, France and the USSR in Moscow. The four powers did not achieve a consensus in the question of the reestablishment of the German central authorities, a German government, the unity of the German economic area or the reparations.
June 14	Order no. 138 of the SMAD about the formation of the German Economic Commission (DWK), the first central zone administration that turns into the provisional government of the GDR in 1949.
September 20-24	2nd party conference of the SED in Berlin. The deputy chairman of the SED, Walter Ulbricht, demands the introduction of the planned economy in the Soviet zone as of 1958 and the conversion of the SED into a "new type of party" after the model of the CPSU (Communist Party of the Soviet Union).
Nov 25 - Dec 15	The failure of the foreign minister's conference in London, final breakdown of the anti-Hitler coalition, begin of the building of the western occupied zones by the western allies without consideration of the Soviet Union.

1948

March 9	The DWK takes over the central coordination and management of the economy in the Soviet zone.
March 20	The Soviet representatives leave the Allied Control Council.
June 21	Currency reform in all three western zones.
June 23	Order of the SMAD about the currency reform in the Soviet zone and all of Berlin.
June 24	Begin of the West Berlin blockade through the Soviet Union and supply of the city through the western allies via the airlift.
June 30	Resolution of the SED about the half-year plan 1948 and the two-year plan 1949/1950: start of the centralist planned economy.
July 3	Formation of the barracked People's Police.
September 6	The non-communist members of the Berlin City Councillor's Meeting convene for the first time in West Berlin.
October 17	Formation of the first "Task Force against Inhumanity" (KgU) by Dr. Rainer Hildebrand.
November 11	The SED city councillors in Berlin and the representatives of the "Democratic Block" form a "Provisional Democratic Magistrate" East Berlin, headed by Friedrich Ebert. The division of Berlin is complete.

1949

March 19	The German People's Council approves the constitution for a "German Democratic Republic".
May 12	End of the Berlin blockade.
October 7	Founding of the German Democratic Republic (GDR), the People's Council

is turned into a provisional People's Chamber, the constitution comes into force, founding of the National Front under the leadership of the SED, on whose unified lists the elections to the People's Chamber take place.

October 11	Wilhelm Pieck becomes president of the GDR.
December 7	Establishment of the High Court of Justice and the Chief Public Prosecutor's Office of the GDR.

1950

January 17	Start of the dissolving of the Soviet internment camps: turnover of the "inmates" to the government organs of the GDR.
January 29	The SED takes action against "bourgeois" politicians that demand free elections with competing lists.
February 8	Formation of the Ministry of National Security; Wilhelm Zaisser becomes minister.
March 2	The provisional government of the GDR refuses the all-German elections demanded by the American High Commissioner as long as occupational forces are stationed.
April 24-29	Political show trial against functionaries of the state and politics already arrested in October of 1949; sentences to long years of imprisonment.
April 26	Start of the "Waldheim Trials".
July 20-24	3rd party conference of the SED in East Berlin; passing of the new party statutes and conversion of the party executive to the Central Committee.
July 25	The first conference of the Central Committee of the SED elects the politburo, the secretariat of the Central Committee and the ZPKK. Walter Ulbricht becomes the secretary general of the CC (Central Committee) of the SED. Only two former social democrats are still members of the politburo.
August 24	Clean-up operation in the SED party executive.
September 29	Admission of the GDR to the "Council for Mutual Economic Aid", COMECON.
December 15	Passing of the "Law for the Protection of Peace" as a criminal law instrument against critics of the People's Chamber.

1951

January 30	Declaration of the government and appeal of the People's Chamber to the Bundestag "Germans around one table" with the suggestion to jointly call in an all-German constituent council.
August 3	Unveiling of the first German memorial for the Soviet dictator Josef Stalin in East Berlin's Stalinallee that was dismantled again in 1961.
September 1	Charge of road tolls for the transit traffic from and to West Berlin by the GDR.

1952

March 10	Surrender of a "Stalin note" to the three western allied forces with the demand for a neutral and unified Germany.
March 25	Rejection of the "Stalin note" by the western powers that see this as a disruptive action against the west-integration of the Federal Republic and in turn demand free elections under UN-supervision.
April 9	Rejection of the answer of the western forces by the Soviet Union.
May 24	East-Berlin show trial ends with a death sentence and long prison sentences.

| May 26 | Decree about a 5 km wide restricted zone along the demarcation line. Start of the compulsory resettlements from the border zone. |

1953

April 20	Price increases for rationed foods.
May 1	No more issue of food ration cards to around two million inhabitants of the GDR – freelancers, entrepreneurs, craftsmen, people working in West Berlin, and others more.
May 17	Decision of the CC of the SED about an increase of the average work rate by an average 10 percent.
May 28	Dissolving of the Soviet Control Commission through the Soviet Union and appointment of a Soviet High Commissioner in Germany. Resolution to raise the average work rate by the Ministry Council.
June 16	Strike of the construction workers in Stalinallee and protests against the increase of the work rate.
June 17	People's uprising in East Berlin and the GDR. Suppression by the Soviet military.
June 18	Further strikes and demonstrations in East German industrial regions.
June 21	Declaration by the CC of the SED that the uprising was a "fascist coup planned for day X" coordinated by West Berlin. Decrease of the average work rate back to the status prior to April 1, 1953.
October 24	Decision of the Ministry Council about the reduction of prices for food and consumer goods as of October 26.

1954

Jan 25 - Feb 18	Foreign minister's conference of the USSR, USA, Great Britain and France in Berlin ends without an agreement about the German question.
March 25	Declaration of the government of the Soviet Union about the recognition of the sovereignty of the GDR.
June 14	Sentencing of several "ringleaders" of the uprising on June 17, 1953.

1955

January 25	The Soviet Union declares the end of the state of war in Germany.
May 1	1st of May demonstrations in East Berlin for the first time with armed units of the fighting troops of the state-owned concerns.
May 11 - 14	Conclusion of the Warsaw Pact
July 18 - 23	No consensus regarding the German problem at the summit meeting of the USSR, USA, Great Britain and France in Geneva.
July 24 - 27	The First Secretary of the Central Committee of the CPSU, Nikita Khrushchev visits the GDR and announces for the first time the new Soviet "Two State Doctrine": reunification only by maintaining the socialist achievements.
September 20	Confirmation of the "full sovereignty" of the GDR through the Soviet Union, abolishment of the office of the High Commissioner, conclusion of a mutual assistance pact with the Soviet Union.
September 26	Resolution of the People's Chamber about the laws concerning "the amendment of the constitution about the protection of the fatherland", the coat of arms and the national flag of the GDR.

| Oct 27 - Nov 16 | Convention of the foreign ministers of the four major powers in Geneva without a consensus regarding the German question. |

1956

January 18	Resolution of the People's Chamber about the establishment of the "National People's Army" (NVA) and the "Ministry of National Defence".
February 13	Participation of an SED delegation headed by Ulbricht and Grotewohl at the 20th party convention of the CPSU in Moscow where Khrushchev called the crimes of Stalin to account in a secret speech. Return of the members of the SED delegation as "declared anti-Stalinists".
Oct 23 – Nov 11	The mass demonstrations in Hungary are expanding to a people's uprising against Stalinism. Despite bitter resistance, the revolution is crushed by Soviet troops.

1957

January 20	Sentencing of a group of Dresden high school students because of "boycott agitation and incitement to uprising"
February 1	Declaration of the CC of the SED about the irrevocable belonging of the GDR to the socialist camp and end of the "thaw".
August 7-14	Khrushchev visits the GDR.
November 1	Erich Mielke is appointed Minister of National Security.
December 11	Resolution of the People's Chamber about a new passport law, which drastically reduces the number of trips to the West. Illegal leaving of the GDR is punished as "escape from the republic". Intensification of the political criminal justice.
December 31	Joining of 25,029 farmers and farm workers to the cooperatives in 1957, establishment of 317 new cooperatives and cooperative cultivation of 25% of the agricultural land.

1958

February 3-6	Resolution of the CC of the SED about "clean-up operations" among full-time functionaries.
July 10-16	Resolution of the party convention of the SED about an economic programme with the goal to surpass the standard of living in the Federal Republic of Germany within three years.
October 27	Declaration by Ulbricht saying that all of Berlin belongs to the territory of the GDR.
November 10	Announcement of the Berlin ultimatum by Khrushchev with the demand to the western forces to leave West Berlin within six months.
November 27	A note by the Soviet Union terminates the occupational statute and demands that West Berlin shall become a demilitarised free city within six months.
December 8	Resolution of the People's Chamber to dissolve the chambers of the states.
December 31	Notes by the three western forces to the Soviet Union in which the one-sided termination of the four-power status of Berlin is rejected.

1959

| May 11 – June 20 | Foreign minister's conference of the USSR, USA, Great Britain and France in |

	Geneva about the German question with observers from the Federal Republic and the GDR ends without results.
June 19	Dispatch of a draft for a non-aggression pact between the GDR and the Federal Republic by the Foreign Ministry of the GDR to the Foreign Office.
August 21	Declaration by Ulbricht that the GDR will catch up with the Federal Republic until 1961 and overtake it.

1960

as of 1960	Installation of mines along the inner-German border.
January 23	Letter by Ulbricht to Federal Chancellor Konrad Adenauer suggesting a plebiscite about disarmament, a peace treaty and German confederation. Demands for a "free city of West Berlin".
March 4	Start of the last phase of compulsory collectivisation.
April 25	Declaration by Ulbricht about the completion of the collectivisation of the agriculture.
September 8	West German citizens are obligated to obtain official approval when entering East Berlin.
September 12	Formation of the National Council of the GDR headed by Ulbricht.

1961

March 28-29	Resolution of the Warsaw Pact states about equipping the GDR with the most modern weapons at their convention in Moscow; Ulbricht suggests closing off West Berlin from East Berlin.
June 3-4	Meeting between the American President John F. Kennedy and Khrushchev in Vienna; renewal of the Berlin ultimatum by Khrushchev.
June 15	Ulbricht demands a neutralisation of West Berlin on the basis of the Soviet memorandum for Germany of June 4 (announcement of a separate peace treaty between the USSR and the GDR and thus the GDR's full sovereign power over the access roads to West Berlin) and declares: "No one intends to build a wall."
July 19-25	In public speeches, Kennedy confirms the "Three Essentials", meaning the vital interests of the West Berlin protective forces: 1) the right of the allies to be present in West Berlin, 2) maintaining free access to Berlin and 3) maintaining the viability of Berlin and the freedom of its people.
August 1	The number of refugees from the GDR is the highest in one month with 30,444 people in July 1961 since the spring of 1953 and October 1955. Increasing agitation in the eastern press against "border commuters", "traffic in human beings" and "enticement".
August 2	1,322 refugees are registered within the last 24 hours in Berlin-Marienfelde. The People's Police confiscate the passports of numerous "border commuters" from the areas along the East German border. Intensified police controls on railway stations and along the sector boundary. "Border commuters" are taken off the trains and sent back or temporarily arrested. The High Court of Justice of the GDR sentences five "traffickers in human beings and spies" to prison sentences between 15 months and two years.
August 3-5	Consultation of the first secretaries of the CCs of the Communist parties of the Warsaw Pact states in Moscow about the conclusion of a peace treaty with Germany and the solving of the West Berlin problem.
August 3	1,100 new refugees are registered in Berlin-Marienfelde. The three city commanders of West Berlin protest with letters with the same wording to the

Soviet commander against the measures of the GDR regime opposite "border commuters" that breach the complete liberty in all of Berlin, contradict the respective agreement and are to be regarded as humanly "absolutely reprehensible".

August 4   Registration of another 1,155 refugees, abrupt increase of the share of "Border commuters" in the number of refugees to 20%. The magistrate of the Soviet sector orders the registration duty for all "border commuters" employed in West Berlin. Effective as of August 1, 1961, they have to pay their rent, electricity, gas and water bills as well as public fees in western DM. Infringements are punished with prison sentences or fines.

August 5   1,283 newly registered refugees in Berlin-Marienfelde. All newspapers in the Soviet occupied sector of Berlin publish reports about evidently controlled "declarations of agreement" by the population regarding the measures against the "border commuters".

August 6-7   3,268 refugees are registered in Berlin-Marienfelde over the weekend.

August 8   1,741 refugees are registered in Berlin-Marienfelde. As the reason for their escape the refugees increasingly state the fear that the escape paths will be blocked. The daily press of the GDR reprints the radio and television speech by Khrushchev in Moscow on August 7 in great detail and utilises it for propaganda purposes. Among other things, Khrushchev had demanded the regulation of the Berlin question but did point out, however, that a blockade of West Berlin in any shape or form was out of the question.

August 9   Another 1,926 refugees are registered in Berlin-Marienfelde. The People's Police steps up its controls in the S-Bahn and U-Bahn trains to West Berlin and constantly arrests people suspected of escaping.

August 10   1,709 refugees are registered in Berlin-Marienfelde. Meeting of the commander of the Soviet forces in Germany with the three West Berlin city commanders.

August 11   The transient camp Berlin-Marienfelde reports another 1,532 registered refugees. The exchange rate reaches a new all-time low: DM 1 west corresponds to 5.10 Marks east. In front of the People's Chamber, the GDR foreign minister declares that the peace treaty is still to come this year. In the session of the People's Chamber, the incumbent prime minister of the GDR, Willi Stoph, announces "new protective measures against traffickers in human beings, enticers and saboteurs", which will result in "certain discomforts" for the citizens. He mentions measures against the traffic from the GDR to the Federal Republic and West Berlin, which is supposedly misused for "traffic in human beings". In a generalised resolution, the People's Chamber orders the Ministry Council to prepare and execute the corresponding measures that lead to a conclusion of the peace treaty and the ending of escapes. Ulbricht meets with the newly commissioned Commander-in-Chief of the Soviet troops stationed in the GDR.

August 12   Apparently in connection with the speech by Stoph and the resolution of the People's Chamber, the number of refugees increases again: Berlin-Marienfelde reports 2,400 new refugees. The train controls by the People's Police are increasing even more, especially on the S-Bahn stations Potsdam, Babelsberg and Griebnitzsee. The trains commuting from Potsdam through West Berlin towards Friedrichstraße are less and less frequented. Travellers wanting to reach the Soviet sector of Berlin from Potsdam are forced to use the "outer ring of Berlin" by the People's Police, after all a detour of 80 km.

August 13   In the early hours of Sunday, units of the People's Police and the People's Army are blocking off the sector boundary between the Soviet sector and West Berlin as of two o' clock in the morning. East Berlin looks like a city under siege. Tank formations, heavily armed police and troop units are taking up position along the sector boundary, reinforced by SED task forces. The "government district" is hermetically sealed off. Upon order of the communist rulers, all inhabitants of East Germany and the GDR are forbidden to enter West Berlin. These measures date back to a directive of the "Warsaw Pact states" that says: "…to introduce such an order at the West Berlin border that is ensured through reliable guarding and a real control." The following is ordered in detail: All inhabitants of the Soviet sector need a permit in order to enter West Berlin. The up to now 88 border crossing points are reduced to 13. "The border commuters" are forbidden to continue working in West Berlin. They either have to report to their last place of employment in the Soviet sector in order to resume their work there or to the government authority in charge. The direct S-Bahn traffic between both halves of the city and from the frontier districts of the GDR to West Berlin is discontinued. The S-Bahn trains that commute in an east-western direction end at Friedrichstraße station. Residents of West Berlin may still enter the Soviet sector after showing their ID-cards. West Berlin trucks may not drive into the Soviet sector. Citizens of the Federal Republic can still obtain day passes for entering the Soviet sector at four issuing offices after presenting their ID-documents. Already in the early morning hours, the border troops and the People's Police are starting to close off roads and squares along the sector boundary from the west sector with barbed wired. Concrete pillars are being erected; obstacles are placed in many spots by digging trenches and tearing up the pavement.

August 14	The military and semi-military units deployed for the closing off are reinforced. Units armed with heavy weapons seal off the entire quarter around the Soviet embassy. Tanks, partially of type T 34, have drawn up at Lustgarten and Marx-Engels-Platz as well as in the side streets of Straße unter den Linden. Brandenburg Gate is blocked off as a crossing points, allegedly because of the "provocations" that occurred there. Now there are only 12 crossing points left. During the course of the day, the communists are deploying water cannons and tear gas bombs in the proximity of Brandenburg Gate against the Berliners demonstrating on the West Berlin side. Concrete pillars and barbed wire fences are set up along the sector boundary at Brandenburg Gate. At night the border demarcation line is illuminated with floodlights. The telephone and telex connections between the GDR and the Federal Republic, and thus also between West Berlin and the GDR are interrupted, only telegrams still pass through.
August 15	Barriers consisting of 1.25 m high concrete slabs are installed in countless places along the sector boundary. The Berliners entering the Soviet sector are subjected to stricter and stricter controls, body searches are conducted on numerous occasions. Additional infantry units take up their position along the sector boundary and armoured scout cars drive up at different places. Barbed wire barriers are also placed around the bases of the tank and infantry units in the Soviet sector, for example at Friedrichstraße station. As the first soldier of the People's Army, Conrad Schumann, jumps across the barbed wire into the west in the district of Wedding. His photo goes around the world.
August 16	The stone and concrete walls along the sector boundary are expanded further, the barrier system is getting denser and denser. Since midnight, the East German border is closed off for residents of the GDR and East Berlin that want to travel to West Germany. West Berlin vehicles are only allowed to pass into the east sector in exceptional cases. Pedestrians are subjected to multiple controls. Tank units and motorised troops are transferred from

	the sector boundary to inner East Berlin. The postal authorities of the GDR take up the interrupted telex traffic with the Federal Republic again.
August 17	The western forces hand over three notes with the same wording in which they denote the closing off of the Berlin Soviet sector through the rulers in the GDR as being illegal and call them a breach of the four power status. In these notes, the Soviet government is held responsible for the encroachments by the GDR authorities and called upon to ensure that the unlawful barriers are removed again. The Soviet radio announces to the population that East Berliners "will not receive any permits to enter West Berlin until the conclusion of the peace treaty". The interzonal traffic from the GDR to the Federal Republic has almost come to a complete standstill. Only 14 travellers from the GDR are counted on this day at all control points. The communist youth association FDJ appeals to its members to sign up for two years of military service.
August 18	In the cover of night, a concrete wall is erected straight across Potsdamer Platz. It is about 1.70 m high. For the first time, armed members of the FDJ are deployed at the sector boundary. As members of the guards have repeatedly escaped in the past days, the most upfront guard positions are increasingly staffed with officers. The total strength of the forces deployed in the Soviet sector is estimated at around 40,000 men. In a special meeting, the German Bundestag in Bonn voices its protest about the barriers and demands their removal.
August 19	The already existing barriers are expanded even further. Doors of houses that are situated in the Soviet sector but have entrances directly towards the west are bricked up. Task forces from state-owned concerns close the SED party offices in East Berlin.
August 20-21	The closing-off measures are continued. Walls with a height of between 2 and 4 metres are erected in various places. Boulevard trees are felled and used for roadblocks. Despite the controls, many West Berliners still visit their relatives and friends in the Soviet sector of Berlin. At the crossing point Wollankstraße alone, the West German police estimates that approximately 7,000 persons passed the sector boundary. The American Vice President Lyndon B. Johnson visits Bonn and West Berlin together with the organiser of the airlift, General Lucius D. Clay, and confirms the determination of the USA to defend the freedom of West Berlin.
August 21	After the entrances of the houses that border directly on West Berlin were already bricked up, the windows facing towards the west are also bricked up. In addition, the People's Police begins enforced evictions. The residents have to pack up their furniture in a hurry and load it onto furniture trucks.
August 22	The erection of the concrete wall continues. In Bernauer Straße, the entrance of Versöhnungskirche, which is situated at the sector boundary in the Soviet sector is bricked up. It was one of the churches whose masses were regularly attended by people form East and West Berlin. Federal Chancellor Adenauer arrives for a visit in West Berlin.
August 23	The authorities of the Soviet sector of Berlin order that West Berliners visiting the Soviet sector also have to apply for a permit from now on. At the same time, the number of border crossings is reduced from 12 to seven. Four of those are crossings reserved for West Berliners, two for visitors from the Federal Republic and one for foreigners. The senate of West Berlin decides not to admit the permit application offices intended by the GDR on West Berlin territory. The GDR Minister of the Interior asks the population "to maintain a distance of 100m to the borders between the capital of the GDR and West Berlin in the interest of their own security". The three western city commanders immediately protest against these new restrictions with a declaration in which

	they accuse the East Berlin authorities of presumptuousness and afterwards deploy armed units for the protection of the sector boundary. The Soviet Union hands over new notes about the Berlin conflict to the ambassadors of the western forces in which they accuse the west of misusing the air corridors.
August 24	Günter Litfin is the first escapee that is shot to death by transport policemen during his attempt to swim from the east to the west through Humboldthafen (harbour). The strict exit conditions also affect the foreigners living in the GDR since August 13 and the foreigners living in East Berlin since August 23. The Ministry Council of the GDR passes a "Decree about Residence Restrictions". According to this decree, a "restriction of residence" can be declared "in special cases on the basis of an adjudication, either additionally to a legal punishment or upon request of the local organs of the state". According to this new regulation, the residence restriction can also be tied to forced labour. The American government issues a declaration to the Soviet note of August 23 in which it turns back the accusations and allegations of the Soviets as being false and warns of an obstruction of the traffic in the air corridors.
August 25	Members of the People's Police are giving off warning shots at the sector boundary to West Berliners for the first time.
August 26	The government of the GDR erects an office each on the "Reichsbahn" grounds of the West Berlin S-Bahn stations Zoo and Westkreuz for the application and issue of residence permits for West Berliners wanting to visit the Soviet sector. The West Berlin senate forbids the operation of these facilities.
August 27	At some points along the sector boundary, a second wall is erected behind the first one that was already built up. In its answering note to the last Soviet note, the British government insists on the free traffic in the air corridors.
August 29	Federal President Heinrich Lübke surprisingly arrives for a visit to Berlin in order to inform himself about the situation. Members of the communist task force shoot an escapee to death at 2:30 pm when he attempted to swim through the Teltow Canal in Berlin-Zehlendorf. The escapee had already reached West Berlin territory.
August 30	Kennedy appoints the former military governor in Germany, General Clay, to his personal envoy in Berlin. The GDR denies the Council of the Evangelical Church in Germany permission to convene in East Berlin.
August 31	The flag of the GDR with the hammer and the sickle is raised on Brandenburg Gate. In his Berlin radio speech, Federal President Lübke declares to the German nation that violence and terror never managed to endure in history. "Those who have seen the sector boundary of Berlin know that it cannot be permanent. It has an unnatural origin."
September 1	Order no. 36/61 of the Ministry of the Interior about the "Fortification Campaign", that decrees the deportation of undesired citizens from the area of the 5 km restricted zone and the 500 m exclusion strip.
September 14	Instructions by the Commander-in-Chief of the Soviet armed forces in Europe to the Ministry of Defence of the GDR on how to secure the border.
September 15	The border troop commando of the National People's Army, formerly the Border Police, become subordinate to the Ministry of National Defence.
October	Berlin: Start of the extension of the wall from a barbed wire barrier to a fortified wall.
October 10-11	Consultation of the CC of the SED and the Ministry Council about the "removal of disruptions" from the economy in order to make it independent of the Federal Republic.
October 17-31	22nd party convention of the CPSU in Moscow: Repeal of the Berlin ultimatum.
October 23-28	Order of the Ministry of the Interior of the GDR that American soldiers in

civilian clothing have to show their ID-cards to the People's Police. As a result, the Americans deploy tanks on October 25. For several days, American and Soviet tanks are facing each other at Checkpoint Charlie until the Soviets give in and withdraw. The uncontrolled access for the western allies to East Berlin is secured again.

November 4	The "Coastal Border Brigade" becomes subordinate to the commando of the NVA naval forces.

1962

January 24	The People's Chamber passes the law about a "general military service", which also applies in East Berlin despite the demilitarised status of Berlin.
June 19	Start of the construction of the second wall behind the first one in East Berlin. This results in the creation of so-called "death strips" in Berlin as well.
July 10	Order about measures for securing and protecting the coastal area of the GDR.
August 17	The East Berlin construction worker Peter Fechter is shot at while attempting to escape across the wall and left lying until he bleeds to death without anyone coming to his aid.
October 19	Dr. Rainer Hildebrandt opens his first exhibition "It happened at the Wall" in Bernauer Straße at the corner of Wolliner Straße.

1963

as of 1963	Begin of the ransoming of GDR-prisoners through the government of the Federal Republic.
June	Harassment by GDR authorities of the road traffic to West Berlin.
June 14	Dr. Rainer Hildebrandt opens his second exhibition in the "House at Checkpoint Charlie" in Friedrichstraße.
June 21	Measures by the GDR-government for the set-up of a "border district" between the GDR and West Berlin
June 26	Kennedy visits West Berlin and is met with great cheer by the population. At the Schöneberg town hall he declares "Ich bin ein Berliner".
July 15	Formulation of the thesis "Change through Approach" for the relations between the Federal Republic and the GDR by the SPD-politician Egon Bahr.
July-September	Renewed harassments by GDR authorities on the interzonal highways to West Berlin.
December 17	First permit treaty between the West Berlin senate and the GDR for West Berliners visiting relatives in East Berlin.

1964

March 13	Regime critic Robert Havemann loses his professorship for physical chemistry at the East Berlin Humboldt-University.
September 1	Confirmation of the exemption from punishment for escapees that left the GDR prior to August 13, 1961 by the People's Chamber.
September 7	Introduction of the "building soldier" as a military service without arms.
September 24	Second permit treaty at the change of the year 1964/1965 year and for Easter and Whitsun 1965.
October 4-5	57 persons manage to escape to the western part of the city through a tunnel in Bernauer Straße in the district of wedding.

October 15	Khrushchev is removed from his functions and succeeded by Leonid Brezhnev.
November 2	First permission for GDR pensioners to visit their relatives in the GDR.
December 1	Introduction of a compulsory currency exchange by the GDR for western visitors.

1965

April	Disruptive Soviet and GDR jet plane flights across West Berlin in order to intimidate the population. Partial blocking of the roads and tracks leading to West Berlin due to a conference of the German Bundestag in West Berlin.
November 25	Third permit treaty for the change of the year 1965/1966.
November 27-30	Visit of the First Secretary of the CPSU Leonid Brezhnev to the GDR.

1966

March 7	Fourth permit treaty for Easter and Whitsun 1966
April 1	Expulsion of Professor Robert Havemann from the German Academy of Sciences in East Berlin.
August 13	Parade of the GDR border troops and SED task forces on the occasion 5th anniversary of the construction of the wall in East Berlin.
October 6	Agreement about the permit office for urgent family matters (hardship cases) that opens on October 10.

1967

| February 20 | The People's Chamber passes the law "about the citizenship of the GDR". |

1968

January 6	Protest of the Soviet Union against the presence of the federation in West Berlin with sessions of the Bundestag committees, the parliamentary coalitions and the cabinet in West Berlin.
January 12	Approval of the new criminal code and a new code of criminal procedure that comes into force on July 1, 1968 by the People's Chamber.
April 6	Referendum about a new GDR constitution, in which the "leading role" of the communist party is established. 94.49 % of all people vote with "yes".
April 9	The new constitution comes into force.
June 10-11	Resolution of the People's Chamber about the introduction of a passport and visa requirement in the travel and transit traffic between the Federal Republic and West Berlin.
June 20	Increase of the compulsory currency exchange.
August 20-21	Forceful suppression of the "Prague Spring" in Czechoslovakia through the invasion of troops from the Warsaw Pact states, among them also the NVA of the GDR.
October 21-28	GDR: Sentencing of demonstrators who had protested against the invasion in Czechoslovakia.
November 12	Announcement of the Brezhnev-Doctrine, meaning the obligation of the sister states to provide military aid in case of a threatening split-off from the Soviet empire.

1969

February	Exchange of letters between Ulbricht and the Foreign Minister of the Federal Republic, Willy Brandt, on the one hand and the West Berlin major, Klaus Schütz, on the other hand.
September 16	Negotiations between the commissioners of the traffic ministries of the Federal Republic and the GDR.
September 19	Negotiations between the commissioners of the German Bundespost and the Ministry for Postal Operations and Telecommunications of the GDR.
October 6	Brezhnev visits East Berlin on the occasion of the 20th anniversary of the GDR.
December 18-20	Exchange of letters between Ulbricht and the Federal President Gustav Heinemann.

1970

March 19	Meeting of Federal Chancellor Willy Brandt and Willi Stoph in Erfurt.
March 26	Start of the negotiations between the four powers about Berlin.
May 21	Meeting of Brandt and Stoph in Kassel.
August 12	Moscow treaty between the Soviet Union and the Federal Republic about the normalisation of the relations and non-aggression.
November 27	Start of the exchange of views between Dr. Michael Kohl, Secretary of State at the Ministry Council of the GDR, and Egon Bahr, Secretary of State at the Federal Chancellery in East Berlin.
December 7	Warsaw treaty between Poland and the Federal Republic about the normalisation of the relations and non-aggression as well as the inviolability of the existing borders.
December 14	Increase of work rates and prices lead to a series of strikes in Poland.
End of the year	Start of the installation of automatic firing devices at the inner-German border, not at the Berlin wall, however.

1971

March 6	Initiation of talks between GDR Secretary of State Kohrt and the West Berlin Senate Director Müller in East Berlin about "mutually interesting questions".
May 3	Request by Ulbricht to remove him from his function as First Secretary of the CC of the SED for reasons of old age. Successor is Erich Honecker.
September 3	Signing of the four-power agreement about Berlin by the three western powers and the Soviet Union, which especially resulted in alleviations in the transit traffic between the Federal Republic and West Berlin.
September 30	Signing of the postal agreement between the Federal Republic and the GDR.
December 17	Signing of the transit agreement between the Federal Republic and the GDR, which comes into force on June 3, 1972.
December 20	Signing of the agreement between the senate of West Berlin and the GDR government about alleviations and improvements in the travel and visitor's traffic as well as the exchange of territory to solve the problem of enclaves.

1972

January 1	Settlement of the road tolls levied individually so far in the transit traffic from and to West Berlin through a flat transit rate paid by the federal government.

January 6	For the first time, Honecker refers to the Federal Republic as a "foreign country".
Easter	In anticipation of the four-powers treaty about Berlin, the first possibility for visits by West Berliners to East Berlin and the GDR in six years. This regulation also applies at Whitsun. Over one million West Berliners take this opportunity.
May 18	The conclusion of the last wave of nationalisations leads to the conversion of companies with a "semi-governmental participation" so far, respectively of small private enterprises to "national property".
May 26	Signing of the traffic contract between the Federal Republic and the GDR that comes into effect on October 17.
June 15	Start of the negotiations about the basic treaty.
October 17	For the first time, GDR-citizens who are not retirees are allowed to travel to the Federal Republic in case of urgent family matters.
December 21	Signing of the basic treaty between the Federal Republic and the GDR in East Berlin. This governs "good neighbourly relations on the basis of equality" and especially brought about humanitarian relief besides non-aggression and the recognition of the inviolability of the borders.

1973

March 5-7	Accreditation of correspondents of the German television stations ARD and ZDF as well as of newspapers and magazines from the Federal Republic in the GDR.
May 28	End of the "Ox Head Campaign", geared against the reception of western broadcasts in the GDR.
September 4	Start of the demarcation of the inner-German border through a joint border commission of the Federal Republic and the GDR.
November 5	Doubling of the compulsory currency exchange.

1974

June 20	Establishment of Permanent Representations of the Federal Republic and the GDR in East Berlin and Bonn.
September 27	Resolution of the People's Chamber about the "Law for the Supplementation and Amendment of the Constitution of the GDR of October 7, 1974" whereby the term "German Nation" was abolished.
October 26	Reduction of the compulsory currency exchange.
December 20	Youths below the age of 16 and retirees are exempt from the compulsory currency exchange.

1975

March 24	Start of negotiations between the GDR and the Federal Republic about the improvement of the transit roads to and from West Berlin.
July 30 – August 1	Conference about Security and Cooperation in Europe (CSCE) in Helsinki. Meeting between the German Chancellor Helmut Schmidt and Erich Honecker.
October 7	Signing of the contract about "friendship, cooperation and mutual assistance between the GDR and the USSR" in Moscow. For the first time, the founding day of the GDR is celebrated as a national holiday.

October 29	Agreement between the Foreign Minister of the GDR and the West Berlin Senator of the Interior about rescue measures at the sector boundary in case of accidents.
December 16	Expulsion of a correspondent accredited in the GDR because of "gross libel" of the GDR.
December 19	Agreement between the Federal Republic and the GDR about the flat transit fee and the improvement of the Autobahn Marienborn-Berlin and other traffic routes from and to West Berlin.

1976

March 30	Signing of the treaty between the Federal Republic and the GDR about postal operations and telecommunications, which comes into force on July 1.
May 1	Michael Gartenschläger, a ransomed former political prisoner in the GDR, is shot to death by a special unit of the MfS on GDR territory where he tried to dismantle an automatic firing device at the inner-German wall.
August 13	15th anniversary of the construction of the wall. 13 of 20 tour busses with members of the "Junge Union" that want to participate in a rally converging on West Berlin are turned back by GDR border patrols under the suspicion of abusing the transit routes.
August 18	Self-burning of the evangelical pastor Oskar Brüsewitz on the market place in Zeitz.
November 16	During a tour of the Federal Republic, the "officials in charge in the GDR" revoke the regime critical songwriter Wolf Biermann's "right to further residence in the GDR".
November 26	Beginning of the 3-year house arrest of Robert Havemann.
December 22	Expulsion of a correspondent accredited in the GDR.

1977

February 17	Confirmation by Honecker in an interview that approximately 10,000 GDR-citizens had applied for an exit permit.
March 1	Levy of road tolls for drives to East Berlin through the GDR.
August 23	Rudolf Bahrow is arrested because of the publication of his regime-critical book "The Alternative" in the Federal Republic. In 1978, he is sentenced to eight years imprisonment and released early in 1979 to the Federal Republic.
October 7	Commotions on East Berlin's Alexanderplatz claim three lives, two of them members of the People's Police.

1978

January 10	Closing of the news office of a news magazine in East Berlin
June 21	Start of the negotiations between the governments of the GDR and the Federal Republic about the construction of an Autobahn between Berlin and Hamburg. Signing of the agreement of November 16.
July 7	Sentencing of the conscientious objector Nico Hübner who refers to the demilitarised status of all of Berlin to five years imprisonment.
September	Introduction of the subject "Military Instruction" at GDR schools with the beginning of the school year for the grades nine and ten.

| November 29 | Signing of the protocol between the Federal Republic and the GDR about the examination, renewal and supplementation of the markings along the inner-German border. |

1979

April 14	The work of western correspondents in the GDR is subject to severe restrictions because now interviews require permission and travels outside of East Berlin need to be reported.
June 28	Resolution of the People's Chamber about the third amendment of the criminal law that comes into force on August 8 and contains substantial intensifications of political criminal law as well as an amendment of the election laws and also includes the direct election of the East Berlin members of the People's Chamber.
September 1	Robert Havemann's ten theses regarding the 30th anniversary of the founding of the GDR with his ideas about urgently necessary political and economic changes.
December 27	Soviet troops invade Afghanistan.

1980

January 1	Discontinuation of the road tolls for drives to East Berlin and payment of an annual flat fee by the Federal Republic in return.
January 22	Arrest of the Soviet civil-rights campaigner Andrej Sacharov in Moscow. He was sent into exile to Gorki without a court sentence.
May 8	Meeting of the Federal Chancellor Schmidt, the Federal President Karl Carstens and the Chairman of the SPD Willy Brandt with Honecker in Belgrade for the memorial ceremony for the president of Yugoslavia Josip Tito who died on May 5.
August	Strikes in numerous Polish cities and founding of the first independent Polish union, "Solidarity", headed by Lech Walesa.
September 19-22	Strike of the West Berlin personnel of the GDR-Reichsbahn.
October 13	The "Gera demands" of Honecker on the Federal Republic concerning the recognition of the status of the GDR as a sovereign state, conversion of the Permanent Representations to embassies, establishment of the Elbe-border in the middle of the river and termination of the central registration office Salzgitter, increase of the compulsory currency exchange to 25 DM, reduction of the number of visitors at Christmas by half.
October 30	Almost complete stop of the private visitor's traffic between Poland and the GDR.

1981

August 13	"Combat demonstrations" in East Berlin on the occasion of the 20th anniversary of the construction of the Berlin wall.
November 20	Re-opening of the Teltow Canal for civil cargo shipping traffic from and to West Berlin.
December 11-13	Meeting between Schmidt and Honecker in the GDR.
December 13	Imposition of martial law in Poland, prohibition of the "Solidarity" union, internment of countless trade unionists.

1982

January 25	Publication of the "Berlin Appeal – Establishing Peace without Weapons" upon an initiative of pastor Rainer Eppelmann who was subsequently arrested for a short time.
February 15	Extension of the catalogue of "urgent family matters" for which GDR-citizens may be granted permission to travel to the west. This increases the number of working citizens allowed to travel.
March 25	Resolution of the People's Chamber about a new military service law.
July 15	Start of the stationing of short-range missiles type SS 21 in the GDR by the Soviet Union.
September 1	Arrest of Roland Jahn during a solidarity rally for "Solidarnosc" in Jena.
November 14	Meeting between Carstens and Honecker in Moscow on the occasion of the funeral ceremony for Brezhnev who died on November 11.
November 20	Opening of the last part of the Autobahn between Berlin and Hamburg.

1983

April 10	Protests in the Federal Republic and worsening of the inner-German climate after the death of the transit traveller Rudolf Burkert during an interrogation at the Autobahn control point Berlin-Drewitz.
June 8	Compulsory expulsion of the member of the Jena peace group Roland Jahn after over 20 members of the "White Circle" were already expelled.
June 29	Approval of a loan by West Germany to the GDR to the amount of 1 billion DM.
July 22	Repeal of the martial law in Poland and amnesty.
July 24	Start of a visit over several days by the Bavarian Minister President Franz Josef Strauß (CSU) to the GDR, meeting with Honecker.
September 1	Police breaks up the human chain between the American and the Soviet embassy in Berlin.
September 15	First meeting between a West Berlin mayor - Richard von Weizsäcker – in East Berlin with a GDR head of state - Honecker.

1984

January 9	Surrender of the S-Bahn installations belonging to the East German Reichsbahn located in West Berlin to the Berlin transport association.
Spring	Unique permission for about 25,000 GDR-citizens to immigrate legally to the Federal Republic.
January 22	GDR-citizens who had applied for asylum at the American embassy receive permission to immigrate.
January 24	GDR-citizens who had fled to the Permanent Representation of the Federal Republic of Germany receive permission to immigrate.
February 14	Death of the Soviet head of state and party Juri Andropov. Meeting of the German Chancellor Helmut Kohl with Honecker on the occasion of the funeral ceremony in Moscow.
April 6	Voluntary return of 35 GDR-citizens who wanted to enforce their immigration via the embassy of the Federal Republic of Germany in Prague to the GDR after they were promised to be able to immigrate soon.
June 27	Temporary closing of the Permanent Representation of the Federal Republic in East Berlin due to its occupation by 55 GDR-citizens who wanted to enforce their relocation to the west this way.

July 25	Loan by the Federal Republic to the amount of 950 million DM to the GDR.
August 1	Reduction of the compulsory currency exchange for pensioners.
October 2	Temporary closing of the West German embassy in Prague after GDR-citizens are trying to enforce their immigration to the west.
End of November	The dismantling of the automatic firing devices along the inner-German border is complete.

1985

January 11	Meeting between the North-Rhine Westphalian minister president Johannes Rau and Honecker in the GDR.
January 15	Again GDR-citizens who want to enforce their immigration to the west flee to the West German embassy in Prague.
February 13	Re-opening of the Semper Opera in Dresden, attended by the Lower Saxon Minister President Ernst Albrecht and former Chancellor Helmut Schmidt.
March 12	Meeting between Kohl and Honecker in Moscow on the occasion of the funeral ceremony for the Soviet head of state and party Konstantin Tshernenko who died on March 10.
End of October	The dismantling of the minefields along the inner-German border is complete.
November 14-16	Visit of the Minister President of Saarland, Oscar Lafontaine, to the GDR upon an invitation of Honecker.

1986

February 9	Expansion of the possibilities to travel in case of urgent family matters.
February 11	Exchange of agents between West Berlin and the GDR on Glienicker Brücke.
February 19-22	Visit of the President of the People's Chamber, Horst Sindemann, to the Federal Republic upon an invitation of the SPD Bundestag group.
April 17-21	Speech by the new Secretary General of the CPSU, Michail Gorbachev, at the party convention of the SED with the demand for self-criticism as an "indispensable condition for the success of a revolutionary party".
April 25	Signing of the first German-German city partnership between Saarlouis and Eisenhüttenstadt.
May 6	Signing of the cultural agreement between the Federal Republic and the GDR.
September 2	Opening of the "Berlin Environment Library".
September 15	Prevention of the Greenpeace protests in East Berlin through security organs.
December 16	Repeal of Sacharov's exile through Gorbachev.

1987

January 27-28	Gorbachev criticises the faults of the past in front of the CC of the CPSU: "We need democracy like the air that we breathe".
June 8	Heavy clashes in East Berlin between youths and the police during a rock concert at the Reichstag, situated in front of the wall in West Berlin.
June 12	Speech of US-President Ronald W. Reagan in front of the Brandenburg Gate on the occasion of his visit to Berlin: "Mr. Gorbachev, open this gate! Mr.Gorbachev, tear down this wall!"
July 1	Drastic reduction of the amount of money that GDR-citizens are allowed to exchange for visits to the west.

July 17	Abolishment of the death penalty and amnesty.
September 5	A demonstration for which there was no notification given of about 1,000 members of the independent peace movement of the GDR in East Berlin. The police does not step in.
September 7-11	Official work visit by Honecker to the Federal Republic.
October 12	Rejection of the Soviet reform policy as a model for the GDR by Honecker in an interview with Belgian journalists.
October 13-14	Rejection of suggested economic reforms by the GDR at the convention of the COMECON-states.
November 14-15	Search of the Environment Library in East Berlin by the Public Prosecutor's Office and the MfS, GDR-wide declarations of solidarity with several persons arrested during the search.

1988

January 17	Participation of numerous demonstrators of independent groups in the official "battle demonstration" in East Berlin to commemorate the murder of Karl Liebknecht and Rosa Luxemburg. About 100 persons from the opposition are arrested.
April-May	Strikes in Poland
September 24	Parade of the "Task Forces of the Working Class" in East Berlin on the occasion of its founding, protest of the three allied city commanders.
November 9-10	The head of the Federal Chancellery, Wolfgang Schäuble, visits East Berlin for consultations.
November 18	Prohibition of the German issue of the Soviet magazine "Sputnik", much read in the GDR, out of fear of the influences of the Soviet reform policies.
December 1-2	Renewed rejection of the Soviet reform policies by Honecker in front of the CC of the SED with the argument "that there is no uniform model that applies to all socialist states."

1989

January 19	On the occasion of a convention of the Thomas-Müntzer-Committee of the GDR, Honecker states: "The wall…will still exist in fifty and even a hundred years if the reasons for its existence have not been eliminated. This is necessary in order to protect our republic from robbers", after criticism of the wall at the Vienna CSCE-conference
February 5	20-year old Chris Gueffroy is shot by GDR-border patrols during his attempt to escape to West Berlin. He is the last escapee that falls victim to the "Regulations for the Use of Firearms" at the wall and the inner-German border.
March 8	After he managed to cross the border, GDR-citizen Winfried Freudenberg crashes to his death during the attempt to escape to West Berlin with a self-made gas balloon. His is the last death registered prior to the fall of the wall. However, numerous deaths of escapees from earlier years first come to light in the West after the opening of the wall.
May 2	Hungary starts the dismantlement of the "Iron Curtain" along the border to Austria. In the subsequent period, masses of GDR-citizens escape. In September, Hungary officially allows GDR-citizens to immigrate. Over 50,000 GDR-citizens take this opportunity until the end of October.
May 7	Municipal elections result in a turnout of 98,78 percent and an approval of 98,85 percent. Members of the opposition speak of a falsification of the elections, which they can partially prove.
May 8	Demonstration in Leipzig against the falsification of the elections.

June 4	Candidates of Solidarnosc win the first partially free elections in Poland.
June 7	Complaint to the State Council about the falsification of the communal elections, temporary arrests.
June 27-28	Honecker visits Moscow. Gorbachev urges reforms in the GDR.
July 7-8	At the summit meeting of the Warsaw pact states, Gorbachev invalidates the "Brezhnev-Doctrine" and stresses "the independent solving of national problems".
August 8	The Permanent Representation of the Federal Republic in East Berlin is closed down after over 100 GDR-citizens willing to leave seek refuge there.
August 19	Mass escapes by approximately 500 GDR-citizens from Hungary to Austria.
August 23	The embassy of the Federal Republic in Prague is closed because of over 100 GDR-citizens that want to enforce their immigration there.
September 8	The GDR-citizens who sought refuge in the Permanent Representation leave it voluntarily after they were promised exemption from punishment and legal council but not a guarantee that they will be allowed to immigrate.
September 19	The embassy of the Federal Republic in Warsaw is closed due to over-crowding with GDR-citizens.
September 25	The "Monday Demonstrations" in Leipzig are getting bigger by the week. On September 25, there were around 8,000 demonstrators, on October 9 about 70,000 and on October 23 about 300,000 who demonstrated for the freedom to travel and democratic reforms in the GDR.
Sept. 30 – Oct. 1	About 6,000 GDR-citizens wanting to immigrate are brought to the Federal Republic from the embassies in Prague and Warsaw and transported with special trains through the GDR.
October 3	The GDR suspends the visa-free visitor's traffic with Czechoslovakia. Up to then, Czechoslovakia was the only country that GDR-citizens were allowed to visit with their ID-cards only.
October 4	Again more than 6,000 GDR-citizens are able to leave the embassy of the Federal Republic in Prague and brought to the Federal Republic by train through the GDR; unrest at the GDR train stations along the way.
October 7-8	The GDR celebrates its 40th anniversary. There are counter-demonstrations both in East Berlin and other cities and over 1,000 persons are arrested. The security forces partially proceed with extreme violence. The protests against the SED do not come to an end in the days to come.
October 18	Egon Krenz succeeds Honecker who is removed from all state and party offices. For his planned politic, Krenz coins the term "Change".
October 27	The state council of the GDR announces an amnesty for all persons sentenced for "illegally leaving the GDR" as well as those arrested in connection with the demonstrations, insofar as they did not commit any violent offences. Again, over 1,000 persons are allowed to leave for West Germany via the embassies of the Federal Republic in Prague and Warsaw.
Oct. 31-Nov. 1	Krenz meets Gorbachev in Moscow. Result: The German reunification is "not on the agenda".
November 1	The visa-free traffic between the GDR and Czechoslovakia is reinstated. As a result, 60,000 GDR-citizens escape via Czechoslovakia to West Germany until the middle of the month.
November 4	The largest demonstration in the history of the GDR. About one million people hit the streets for democratic reforms in East Berlin.
November 7	The Ministry Council of the GDR resigns.
November 8	The entire politburo of the GDR resigns, but Krenz is confirmed as Secretary General.
November 9	Around 7 am, member of the politburo Günter Schabowski announces the opening of the borders in passing. Already a few hours later, the first East

	Berliners are in West Berlin and there are unimaginable scenes of joy. As of immediately, all GDR-citizens are free to leave and travel. In the following days, millions of GDR-citizens visit the Federal Republic and West Berlin, countless new border crossing points are established.
November 13	Hans Modrow, up to then the Dresden district head of the SED, is elected the new Minister President of the GDR by the People's Chamber.
November 17	The head of the government Hans Modrow suggests a "contractual commu- nity" to the Federal Republic. The MfS is renamed to "Office for National Security".
November 23	Initiation of the party proceedings against Erich Honecker.
December 3	Under pressure of the mass demonstrations, the entire politburo of the SED including Egon Krenz resigns.
December 6	Krenz also resigns his office as head of the State Council of the GDR. His successor is Manfred Gerlach, head of the Liberal Democratic Party of Germany (LDPD). The state council passes another amnesty.
December 7	The "talks at the round table" between government parties and representa- tives of the different opposition groups begin in the GDR.
December 9	At a special party convention of the SED, the East Berlin lawyer Gregor Gysi is elected as the new chairman.
December 11	New mass demonstrations in the GDR, especially in Leipzig. The call "Ger- many, united Fatherland" comes more and more into the foreground.
December 18	The "round table" declares itself in favour of a "contractual community" between the GDR and the federal government.
December 19-20	Federal Chancellor Kohl visits the GDR. Modrow turns down Kohl's 10-point programme and insists on the sovereignty of the GDR.
December 22	Opening of a border crossing point for pedestrians at Brandenburg Gate.
December 24	Repeal of the visa requirement as well as the compulsory currency exchange for travels to the GDR and East Berlin.
December 31	Hundreds of thousand people effusively celebrate the change of the year at the "New Year's Eve celebration of the century" at Brandenburg Gate.

1990

January 3	Following an appeal of the SED-PDS for a "battle demonstration", 250,000 people demonstrate against "neo-fascism and "anti-Sovietism" in the East Berlin district of Treptow at the Soviet memorial besmirched by unknown persons. Opposition groups that participate in the round table talks protest against the planned establishment of an intelligence service and an organ for the protection of the constitution prior to the elections to the People's Chamber. In the district of Schwerin, construction workers start to dismantle the security installations at the wall.
January 12	A government crisis in the GDR can be settled after Minister President Modrow abstains from establishing an office for the protection of the constitution in the place of the disbanded National Security Service and its successor organisation "Office for National Security".
January 15	Several thousand demonstrators in East Berlin invade the headquarters of the former National Security Service. In Leipzig, over 100,000 people demonstrate for the unity of Germany.
January 23	GDR border troops start replacing the wall with a fence. Altogether, 320 m of wall are to be removed at Leuschnerdamm, "apparently because of the especially colourful graffiti, which the GDR foreign trade company Limex is now selling to affluent interested persons", reported the West Berlin newspaper "Der Tagesspiegel" on January 24.

January 28	The fractions represented at the round table decide to bring the elections for the People's Chamber forward to March 18.
January 29	The former head of state and party, Erich Honecker, is moved from the hospital to the remand prison Rummelsburg (East Berlin), One day later he is released again because of unfitness to be kept in prison for health reasons and brought to Lobetal (district of Bernau) to the ecclesiastical nursing home there.
January 30	Modrow arrives for talks with Gorbachev in Moscow. The head of the SED-PDS now also advocates the German unity.
February 1	GDR Minister President Modrow presents a phased plan for a unified Germany under the motto "For Germany, united Fatherland"
February 4	After a resolution of the executive party committee, the former SED (by now SED-PDS) from now on calls itself PDS only (Party of Democratic Socialism).
February 6	Federal Chancellor Kohl announces in Bonn the offer of immediate negotiations concerning an economic and currency union.
February 10	After talks with Gorbachev in Moscow, Kohl declares that the USSR regards the German unification as a matter that can only be decided by the Germans alone.
February 13	Chancellor Kohl and GDR Minister President Modrow agree in Bonn upon initial steps for the reunification of the two German states.
February 19	The round table rejects a reunification according to article 23 of the constitution and also rejects the membership of the future reunited Germany in the NATO. Between the Reichstag and Brandenburg Gate, GDR border troops begin dismantling the wall. Instead of the wall, intentions are to erect a fence with a height of 1.50 m on the stretch up to Checkpoint Charlie.
March 14	Beginning of the "Two plus Four" negotiations (negotiations between the victorious powers of the Second World War with the two German states) on a civil servant level in Bonn about the outer aspects of the German unification.
March 16	The stream of migrants from the GDR continues undiminished. Altogether 14,772 migrants have reported since the beginning of the year.
March 18	The "Alliance for Germany" wins the first free elections in the GDR with 48.15% (CDU: 40.91%, DSU 6.32%, DA 0.92%). The SPD receives 21.84%, the PDS 16.33%. The citizen's movements, united in the "Alliance 90" merely receive 2.9%.
March 28	French President Mitterand and the British Prime Minister Margaret Thatcher openly speak up for a reunification of Germany.
April 3	Honecker is moved from the vicarage Lobetal to a Soviet military hospital in Beelitz (district of Potsdam).
April 7	Opening of the border crossing point Brunnenstraße at the corner of Bernauer Straße
April 12	For the first time since 1946, regular busses again drive across the urban border. At Easter (April 15-16), there are 43 possibilities to leave the western part of the city. In the GDR, the "Alliance for Germany", the SPD and the Liberal Party form a grand coalition. The head of the CDU, Lothar de Maizière is elected to Minister President by the People's Chamber.
April 24	Kohl and de Maizière agree the introduction of an economic, currency and social union starting at July 2nd.
April 28	The EC-summit agrees to the reunification of Germany. With the aid of West-Berlin companies, construction units of the National People's Army start to tear down the wall in front of Brandenburg Gate.
May 5	Start of the conference of the foreign ministers of the four victorious powers of the Second World War as well as the Federal Republic and the GDR about the outer conditions of the German unity in Bonn ("Two plus Four" talks, first German conference since 1959). Main topics: the military status of the united

	Germany, the Polish western border, and replacement of the allied rights in Germany.
May 6	The municipal elections in the GDR confirm the balance of power of the elections to the People's Chamber of March 18. The SPD becomes the strongest party in East Berlin and provides the mayor from now on.
May 18	Signing of the international treaty for the currency, economic and social union between the two German states in Bonn.
June 3	The American President George Bush and Gorbachev agree about the German unity.
June 9	The reservations of the western allies of May 12 1949 regarding the full right to vote of the West Berlin representatives in the Bundestag and the Federal Council are withdrawn.
June 12	Almost 42 years after the division of the city's administration, the East German Magistrate and the Senate of Berlin meet in the "Rote Rathaus" (Red Town Hall) in East Berlin for the first joint session and decide to initially restore 86 road connections separated by the wall besides passing a declaration about the restoration of the city's unity.
June 13	The final dismantling of the wall starts in Bernauer Straße.
June 21	Both the Bundestag and the People's Chamber agree to the German-German international treaty about the currency, economic and social union.
June 22	With the exception of Saarland and Lower Saxony, the Federal Council agrees to the German-German international treaty. The border crossing of the western allies, Checkpoint Charlie – the symbol of Cold War, is dismantled in a solemn celebration in the presence of the foreign ministers of the four victorious forces of the Second World War and the major Ingrid Stahmer as well as that of East Berlin mayor Tino Schwierzina.
June 27	Government agreement between the Federal Republic and the GDR about the abolishment of the controls at the inner-German border and in Berlin as of July 1, 1990.
June 29	Federal President Richard von Weizsäcker becomes the first honorary citizen since the division of the city administration at the end of 1948.
June 30	At the end of the day, the border controls at the inner-German border and in Berlin are abolished and the currency, economic and social union comes into force. Seven U-Bahn stations that are still closed in East Berlin are reopened and the Berlin public transport system grows together even more. In addition, the registration procedure for transient GDR-citizens that relocate to the Federal Republic is abolished.
July 6	Start of the negotiations about the unification contract.
July 16	In the Caucasus, Kohl and Gorbachev agree upon the NATO-membership of the united Germany.
July 22	The People's Chamber decides upon the reinstatement of the states abolished in 1952.
August 22	With the necessary two-thirds majority, the People's Chamber passes the election contract as the basis for the first all-German elections on December 12, 1990.
August 23	The People's Chamber decides joining the Federal Republic on October 3, 1990.
August 31	The German-German unification contract is concluded in East Berlin.
September 10	Agreement about the withdrawal of the Soviet troops.
September 12	Conclusion of the "Two plus Four" talks. Signing of the contract "about the final regulation with regards to Germany".
September 19	The GDR appoints Joachim Gauck as the special envoy for handling the MfS-files.
September 20	The Bundestag and the People's Chamber adopt the unification contract.

September 24	The GDR resigns from the Warsaw Pact.
October 1	In New York, the four victorious powers of the Second World War declare the reserved rights and responsibilities for Germany and Berlin as suspended as a whole and factually grant united Germany full sovereignty. The contract finally comes into force on March 15, 1991, after the Soviet Union as the last state in the contract has deposited the ratification certificate with the all-German government.
October 2	Dissolving of the People's Chamber in the GDR.
October 2/3	"Reunification Celebration" and state ceremony. Start of the governmental union as of October 3, 1990, 0:00 AM. Hoisting of the black-red-gold federal flag at Platz der Republik in front of the Reichstag.

The wall near „Stadion der Weltjugend", Berlin-Mitte, June 1990

Biography of the founder of the Wall Museum - Museum House at Checkpoint Charlie, Dr. Rainer Hildebrandt

1914	Born in Stuttgart on December 14.
	Father: Hans Hildebrandt, art historian TU Stuttgart (first monographies about Alexander Archipenko and Oskar Schlemmer; lost his university chair during the NS-regime as his mother is of Jewish decent).
	Mother: Lily Hildebrandt, painter (master student of Adolf Hölzel; was prohibited to paint during the NS-regime due to her non-Arian descent).
	Childhood and youth in Stuttgart.
1934	Abitur.
	April to August: Reich labor service.
1934-1935	University student apprentice at "Fortuna-Werke", Bad Cannstatt.
1935-1936	Autumn to spring: Work – partially already independently – in the laboratory for applied physics at Robert Bosch AG., Stuttgart.
1936	First semester (summer semester) at Technische Hochschule Stuttgart, physics.
	Relocation to Berlin.
1936-1938	August to February: Student worker at Telefunken.
1938	Since March employment as engineer at Telefunken. Independent work, registration of patents for Telefunken as well as registration of several patents outside his work field. Left at his own request in September 1938.
1939-1940	Employment in the invention department at Radio-Löwe AG Berlin.
	Publications since 1938: numerous contributions about electroacoustic in the industry journals "Funktechnische Monatshefte", "Funk" and "Funkschau".
1937-1939	Study of physics at Technische Hochschule Charlottenburg then at the Berlin University.
since 1939	Expansion of the university studies to philosophy, psychology, political science and national economy.
	First encounter with Albrecht Haushofer.
1942	Promotion at Friedrich-Wilhelm-University Berlin about work psychology taught by Prof. Rupp and Eduard Spranger, minor in philosophy and physics; student and friend of Albrecht Haushofer, and also his "mailman"; friendship with Horst Heilmann, the loyal assistant of Harro Schulze-Boysen; encounter between Haushofer and Schulze-Boysen in Rainer Hildebrandt's apartment.
	Preparatory work for a new larger publication in the field of political science.
	In summer: Conscription to the Wehrmacht, training in Schneidemühl. As of the late summer of 1942, work at a news-interpreting department in Meißen.
1943	In January transfer back to Schneidemühl, escape from the troop after a denunciation and subsequent arrest.
1944	Second arrest, again because of "Subversion of the armed forces" (altogether 17 months).
since the end of the war	Journalistic activities, initially about Walther Rathenau; publication of "Moabiter Sonette" by Albrecht Haushofer in 1946, first book publication "We are the Last Ones. About the life of the resistance fighter Albrecht Haushofer and his friends" in 1948.
1948	Founding of the "Task force against inhumanity" (KgU), an organization

	that established a tracing service for missing prisoners, informed about NKWD and GDR imprisonment but also engaged in resistance against the regime in the Soviet Occupied Zone/GDR.
1951	Five-month journey with 40 lectures in the USA, especially about the prison system, judiciary and resistance in the GDR.
1952	Resignation from the KgU after the group carried out acts of sabotage under the leadership of Ernst Tillich. Founding of "Freiheitsbund für Deutsch-Russische Freundschaft" (Freedom Alliance for German-Russian Friendship), honorary chairman Ernst Reuter, co-chairman Alexander Truschnowitsch, who was forcefully abducted and murdered.
until 1961	Mainly journalistic activities, book publications: "Als die Fesseln fielen" (the revolt on June 17), also published in the USA ("The Explosion") and in Italian. Numerous articles, among others in "Les temps modernes", as well as regular publications about human rights topics (1948 until 1995) and especially the GDR in "Tagesspiegel" newspaper. Editor-in-chief of the magazine by "Deutsche Liga für Menschenrechte" [German Human Rights League]. Research assignments for the Federal Ministry of All-German Questions.
1961	In December: First press conference with refugees from the GDR.
October 19, 1962	Inauguration of the exhibition "It happened at the Wall" in Wolliner Straße, prepared together with former GDR prisoners, refugees and students.
1963	In June: Registration of the Registered Association "Arbeitsgemeinschaft 13. August" (Work Group August 13); since then executive chairman of the association.
June 14, 1963	Inauguration of "Haus am Checkpoint Charlie"; since then its director.
1971	Integration of the exhibition in Wolliner Straße into "Haus am Checkpoint Charlie".
1973	Inauguration of the exhibition "Maler interpretieren DIE MAUER" (Painters interpret the Wall).
1976	Inauguration of the exhibition "BERLIN – Von der Frontstadt zur Brücke Europas" (BERLIN – from the Frontline City to the Bridge to Europe).
1984	Inauguration of the exhibition "VON GANDHI BIS WALESA – Gewaltfreier Kampf für Menschenrechte" (FROM GANDHI TO WALESA – The Non-Violent Fight for Human Rights).
1987	Inauguration of the building extension Friedrichstraße 43 (ground floor and 1st floor).
1989	98 performances of the theater play "R wie Rosa" (escape with a US uniform).
1990-1995	Conception and organization of the touring exhibition "Ende der Berliner Mauer – Anfang des neuen Europa" (The End of the Berlin Wall - The Beginning of the New Europe) through Easter Europe and Israel.
1991-1994	Conception and organization of the touring exhibition "BREAKTHROUGH – The Fight for Freedom at the Berlin Wall" through the USA together with the German Historical Museum.
1991	Initiation and beginning of the talks between perpetrators and victims between former prisoners and members of the Stasi.
1999	Inauguration of the building extension Friedrichstraße 45 (second floor).
2000	In August: Inauguration of the true-to-original replica of the first allied control barracks in Friedrichstraße.
2004	Dr. Rainer Hildebandt passes away in the early hours of 9th January.

Distinctions for Dr. Rainer Hildebrandt

- 1992 Order of Merit of the State of Berlin
- 1994 Order of Merit of the Federal Republic
- 1998 Imre-Nagy Badge

Publications of Rainer Hildebrandt (Selection)

Brochures:
- KgU: Berichte aus Mitteldeutschland
- Was lehrte der 17. Juni? Eine Denkschrift
- Die Mauer
- Vom "13. August" zur "Modernen Grenze"
- 15 Jahre Mauer
- Wie sie die Mauer sehen
- Die gravierendsten Menschenrechtsverletzungen in der DDR
- Die gravierendsten Verletzungen von Arbeitsrechten in der DDR
- Ich war Grenzaufklärer
- Das Selbstschußgerät SM 70
- Probleme zur Realisierbarkeit eines schrittweisen Abbaus des Schießbefehls
- Claus Schenk Graf von Stauffenberg 1907 - 1944. Aus Anlaß des 80. Geburtstages
- Sacharow und die Menschenrechte, Plakatausstellung
- Nimm mich, Zeus
- Libida und Libido
- R wie Rosa (Bühnenstück, 98 Aufführungen im Haus am Checkpoint Charlie)
- 130 Jahre Zuchthaus

Books:
- Wir sind die Letzten
- 2 x 2 = 8
- Kontrollpunkt Kohlhasenbrück
- Berlin Friedrichstraße, 20.53 Uhr
- Es geschah an der Mauer
- Die Mauer spricht
- Die Mauer - Faszination der Fotokunst
- Als die Fesseln fielen
- Der 17. Juni
- Von Gandhi bis Walesa - Gewaltfreier Kampf für Menschenrechte
- Berlin - Von der Frontstadt zur Brücke Europas
- Berlin - Ich liebe Dich
- Wo Weltgeschichte sich manifestiert
- Geteilte Interpretationen – Maler sehen die Mauer
- Maler interpretieren die Mauer
- Kurt Mühlenhaupt – Maler der Menschenliebe
- Lusici: Weg-Zeichen
- Grigorjew: Erotische Zeichnungen
- Die Freiheit hat schon begonnen

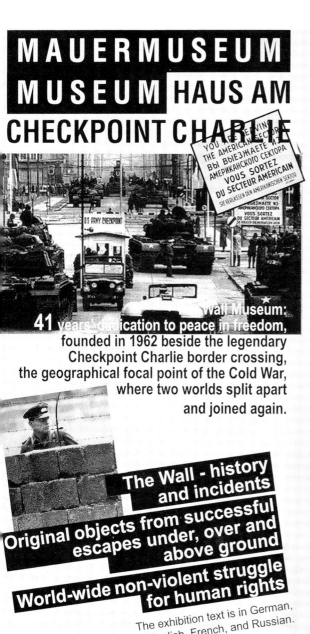

MAUERMUSEUM
MUSEUM HAUS AM
CHECKPOINT CHARLIE

**Wall Museum:
41 years' dedication to peace in freedom,
founded in 1962 beside the legendary
Checkpoint Charlie border crossing,
the geographical focal point of the Cold War,
where two worlds split apart
and joined again.**

**The Wall - history
and incidents**

**Original objects from successful
escapes under, over and
above ground**

**World-wide non-violent struggle
for human rights**

*The exhibition text is in German,
English, French, and Russian.*

**Open every day of the year
from 9.00 until 22.00**

Origin
Developmen
Futur

by Rainer Hildebran
Founder and Director of t
Museum until his dea
14.12.1914 - 09.01.20

The first exhibition opened on the 19 October 1962 in an apartment with only two and a half rooms in famous Bernauer Straße. The street was divided along its whole length; the buildings in the east had been vacated and their windows were bricked up. We suggested that tourists be thankful to those border guards who do not shoot to kill: "See through the uniform!" Some guards saw that we understood, and after their own escapes came to work with us.

The large number of visitors encouraged us to look for new premises: on 14 June 1963 the "Haus am Checkpoint Charlie" was opened and became an island of freedom right next to the border. From here, through a small window, escape helpers could observe all movements at the border crossing; escapees were always welcome and supported, escape plans were worked out, and injustice in the GDR was always fought against.

The aim was to document the "best border security system in the world" (GDR armed forces general Karl-Heinz Hoffmann) and the support of the protecting powers — until the tank confrontation between the USA/USSR. Further exhibitions followed: 1973 "Artists interpret THE WALL", 1976: "Berlin - from a front-line city to Europe's bridge", 1984: "FROM

GANDHI TO WALESA - non-vio
lent struggle for human rights".

Because of our friendly conta
with escape helpers we got hot-
balloons, escape cars, chairlifts
and a small submarine. We are
grateful to resistance activists fc
a spring gun for the dismantling
which they had risked their lives
and a piece of the wall's tubular
top-cladding, knocked off by "w
runner" John Runnings.

We can also call ourselves
the first museum of internationa
non-violent protest. Our exhibit:
include: The Charta 77 typewrit
the hectograph of the illegal pe
odical "Umweltblätter" ("Enviror
mental Pages"), Mahatma Gan
dhi's diary and sandals and fro
Elena Bonner the death mask c
her partner Andrei Sacharov.

There are over a hundred mi
tary museums in the world. But
an epoch of growing responsib
for our planet we can be sure t
more museums of internationa
non-violent protest will be esta
lished. "The world is so well bu
that against every injustice the
are stronger, vanquishing force
...From every injustice arises
justice, from every untruth truth
from darkness light." – Words c
Mahatma Gandhi.

THE WALL
from 13 August 1961
to its fall

BERLIN
from a front-line city
to the bridge of Europe

The exhibition presents the history of both parts of the divided city - their contrasts and similarities - as from the end of World War II. The presentation is always "two-sided" - events in West Berlin are seen in relation to those in the East: Berlin in ruins, rebuilding, blockade and airlift, Ernst Reuter's appeal to the world (1948): "Look to this city and recognise that you must not abandon it and its people, that you cannot abandon it!"

17 June 1953: almost everywhere in the GDR the population is in revolt. The uprising is brutally put down with the help of Soviet tanks.

Further stages in the exhibition show the building of the Wall, the Four Powers Agreement, the 750th anniversary celebrations, the fall of the Wall and the German reunification.

August 1961: all around st Berlin, armed military units e GDR hermetically seal off city. The erection of the wall ns...

November 1989: politburo ber Günter Schabowski announces the decision of the GDR ernment that "travel abroad rivate reasons may be unitionally applied for."
w hours later border concan no longer deal with rowds and let the people gh...
ese two historic dates mark orner-stones of our exhibiabout the Berlin Wall, the ry of which is presented by ns of photographs and texts. erous original objects from essful escapes demonstrate ourage and creativity of the bees. Photos and objects the development of the 's border security system,

from the first hollow blocks to the Wall ot the fourth-generation, the L-shaped segments of which became the longest concrete canvas in the world. A spring gun for the dismantling of which they had risked their lives, and other elements of the former "border security system" surrounding a city and a country illustrate the Wall's historic uniqueness.

THE WALL becomes a challenge: from GDR citizens, who call for freedom of movement by simply writing "§ 13" (paragraph 13 of the UN Charter) on their chests, to US citizen John Runnings, who - sitting astride the wall - is hammering off a piece.

It happened at
CHECKPOINT CHARLIE

Friedrichstr. 43-45
D-10969 Berlin-Kreuzberg

Tel.: (030) 25 37 25-0
Fax: (030) 251 20 75

Postal address:
Postfach 61 02 26
D-10923 Berlin

MAUERMUSEUM
MUSEUM HAUS A
CHECKPOINT CHARL

Open every da
of the ye
from 9.00 until 22.

Public transpo
Underground line 6, Kochstra
Underground line 2, Stadtmi
Bus 1

Checkpoint Charlie was the most well-known border crossing between East and West. In October 1961 American and Russian tanks faced each other here, when the USA intervened to defend the fundamental rights of Berlin's special status.

Again and again, Checkpoint Charlie is the scene of demonstrations. Escape attempts are either successful (eg. in an *Isetta*, a small *car* reconstructed for escape purposes is displayed in the museum) or fail just in front of the the white borderline. On 17 August 1962, Peter Fechter bleeds to death before the eyes of the world.

Finally, on 22 June 1990, in the presence of the foreign ministers of the four victorious powers of World War II and both German states, Checkpoint Charlie is demolished in a solemn ceremony.

he GDR border security system
Ring around Berlin (West)"

s of 31 July 1989

tal length of the "Ring around Berlin (West)" – this:	155.0 km
tween Berlin (West) and Berlin (East)	43.1 km
tween Berlin (West) and the GDR	111.9 km
ncrete plate wall with tubular o-cladding or inserted tubes 5 - 4.2m; only near the border, in the rear area th often the same wall or a wall consisting of ee boards not included)	106.0 km
tal fencing	66.5 km
servation towers	302
nkers	20
g-runs	259
tor vehicle trenches	105.5 km
ctric contact or signal fencing	127.5 km
itary roadway	124.3 km

asurements of a wall segment:

ight	3.60 m
dth	1.20 m
eadth at the base	2.10 m
ll thickness	0.2 m below; 0.1 m on top
ight	2.6 tons
terial	thick reinforced concrete

ng around Berlin (West)" (13.08.61 - 09.11.89)
alities and Escape Attempts:

ccessful escape attempts	5,075
hese members of armed brigades	574
ims	190
al fatalities of the GDR border regime 48-1989; German-German border, ic Sea, other Eastern Block States included)	1,067

This exhibition - including 14 loans from the Gandhi family, the typewriter belonging to "Charta 77" from the former Czechoslovakia, the hectograph of the illegal periodical "Umwelt-blätter" ("Environmental Pages") from the GDR - can be called the first exhibition of international non-violent protest.

Examples from various countries show how justice was achieved without wrongdoing with either humour or non-violent demonstrations. Included are the "Monday Demonstrations" in Leipzig and the demonstration on "4 November" in East Berlin, followed by the fall of the Berlin Wall five days later, and finally Moscow's "Three Days in August": In the museum, the 50 metres long, white, blue and red flag can be seen behind which Moscow's citizens gathered to defeat the communists' coup d'état.

Artists
interpret
THE WALL

Between 1961 and 1989 more than 5,000 people were able to escape across the Berlin Wall. In the course of time the aids they used to overcome the increasingly perfected GDR border security system became more and more inventive, and many of them have found their way into the museum's collection: several reconstructed cars, a mini submarine with which an escapee dragged himself along in the Baltic Sea, hot-air balloons and home-made motor-powered kites equipped with a Trabant engine or the tank of a

Java motorbike. People also escaped hidden in loudspeakers, in a radiogram.

Full documentation is availab on numerous escape tunnels. T most successful of them enable 57 people to reach West-Berlin on two evenings in October 196 In addition to many photograph of the tunnel, the car in which the earth masses were transported also on view. For this donation are grateful to one of the escap helpers, Reinhard Furrer, who lateron became one of the first Germans in space and who die in 1995 in a plane crash.

"It is only because artists and poets have borne witness that we can understand past hopes and recognise their perspectives for the future."

These words by the philosopher Ernst Bloch are the introductory motto to our art exhibition. It not only presents the at first rarely occurring portrayals of the Berlin Wall in visual art (Horst Strempel, Roger Loewig, Gisela Breitling), but also, among others, works by Johannes Grützke, Matthias Koeppel and Karl Oppermann appearing lateron.

The exhibition, which we are continually able to extend thanks to the kind support of the foundation "Stiftung Deutsche Klassenlotterie Berlin", is not only a comprehensive overview of artistic portrayals of the Wall, it also covers a wide range of artistic com-

mitment to human rights as a whole.

Works can be seen by numerous internationally renowned artists such as Bill Brussilowski, Bulatow, Roseline Granet, Hajek, Heiliger, Hannah Höch, Kolar, Kyncl, Makarov, Masson, Penck, Reuter, Rischar and Tapies. In the end, photographs and objects can only inform, but artists can exemplify how a particular time was experienced.

Film shows:

daily from 9.00-22.00

Videos on subjects from the exhibitions ("17 June", Escape by tunnel, John Runnings on the Wall, The End of the Wall, Rostropowitsch Plays at Checkpoint Charlie; films on passive resistance: Czechoslovakia, Moscow)

**Feature Films
and Documentary Films**

9:30, 11:30, 13:30, 15:30, 17:30 hours every day

"With the Wind to the West"
19:30 hours every day
"My Struggle"

**Lectures on
Exhibition Subjects**
with appointment please

Guided Tours through the Museum and to the Wall
with appointment please

Library:

public reference library focusing post-war history, the Cold War, propaganda, GDR, the BERLIN WALL and border security system, state security, reappraisal of the past. Uprisings and revolutions Eastern Europe: "17 June" 1953, 1980 (Poland, Solidarnosc), peaceful revolutions 1989. Non-violent protest world-wide.

Library opening times
Mondays to Fridays
10.00 to 17:00 h
and upon prior appointment

Cafeteria
open daily from 09:00 to 22:00 h

Admission:
Adults **9,50 €**
School and university students etc.
5,50 €
Groups of more than 10 persons,
5,50 € per person
(booking in advance is not necessary)

Wardrobe, luggage

Wardrobe	free
Lockers	free
Lockers for valuables	free

**Open every day
of the year
from 9:00 until 22:00 h**

Friedrichstraße 43-45
D-10969 Berlin-Kreuzberg

Postal address:
Postfach 61 02 26
D-10923 Berlin

Phone: (030) 25 37 25-0
Fax: (030) 251 20 75

E-Mail:
info@mauermuseum.de
Internet:
www.mauermuseum.de

Books by "Haus am Checkpoint Charlie Publications"

IT HAPPENED AT THE WALL
224 p., 227 photos, 20th extd. ed.
2003 (hitherto 1,110,000),
in Eng., Fr., Sp., It.
ISBN3-922484-50-6, **12,50 €**

**FROM GANDHI TO WALESA
Non-violent struggle for human rights**
304 p., 369 photos, in Engl., Fr.
ISBN 3-922484-33-6, **10,50 €**

German Post-War History in Selected Articles by Rainer Hildebrandt 1949-1993
192 p., 220 photos
ISBN 3-922484-45-X, **12,50 €**

THE WALL, Figures, Data
144 p., 55 photos
ISBN 3-922484-46-8, **12,50 €**

Please request our catalogue for information about other books available from "Haus am Checkpoint Charlie Publications" ("17 June" uprising, Berlin Wall, GDR border security system, Artists Interpret THE WALL, Stasi).

Also available in the museum´s shop:
- T-shirts, Art-shirts
  (in limited numbers)
- original pieces of the Wall
- Postcards, posters
- Slides
- Leporello "Along the Wall" consisting of 33 postcards of wall-painting; total length almost 5 metres
- Souvenirs for friends and collectors

List of Abbreviations

FRG	Federal Republic of Germany
CDU	Christian-Democratic Union of Germany
DA	"Demokratischer Aufbruch" (Democratic Awakening)
GDR	German Democratic Republic
DSU	German Social Union
GEC	German Economic Commission
FDGB	Freier Deutscher Gewerkschaftsbund
FDJ	"Freie Deutsche Jugend" (GDR youth organisation)
KgU	„Kampfgruppe gegen Unmenschlichkeit" (Task Force against Inhumanity)
KPD	German Communist Party
CSCE	Conference for Security and Cooperation in Europe
LDP(D)	Liberal-Democratic Party (Germany)
LPG	GDR-cooperative
MfS	Ministry of National Security
NVA	National People's Army
PDS	Party of Democratic Socialism
PGH	Crafts cooperative
RGW	Council for Mutual Economic Aid (COMECON)
SOZ	Soviet Occupational Zone
SED	Socialist Unity Party of Germany
SMAD	Soviet Military Administration in Germany
SPD	Socialist Party of Germany
SSD	State Security Service
Stasi	State Security Service
USSR	Union of Soviet Socialist Republics
UNO	United Nations Organisation
USA	United States of America
ZK	Central Committee
ZPKK	Central Party Control Commission of the SED